CONTENTS

To Clemen [handwritten inscription]

PENGUIN BOOKS

SIMONE DE BEAUVOIR

Lisa Appignanesi is Deputy Director of the Institute of Contemporary Arts and editor of the *Documents* series. She has written several books, fiction and non-fiction, including a study of 'femininity' in the works of Henry James, Marcel Proust and Robert Musil, and on the history of cabaret. Born in Poland, brought up in France and Canada, she now lives in London with her two children and companion.

LIVES OF MODERN WOMEN

General Editor: Emma Tennant

Lives of Modern Women is a series of short biographical portraits by distinguished writers of women whose ideas, struggles and creative talents have made a significant contribution to the way we think and live now.

It is hoped that both the fascination of comparing the aims, ideals, set-backs and achievements of those who confronted and contributed to a world in transition, and the high quality of writing and insight will encourage the reader to delve further into the lives and work of some of this century's most extraordinary and necessary women.

Lisa Appignanesi

Simone de Beauvoir

Penguin Books

Penguin Books Ltd, 27 Wrights Lane, London W8 5TZ (Publishing and Editorial)
and Harmondsworth, Middlesex, England (Distribution and Warehouse)
Viking Penguin Inc., 40 West 23rd Street, New York, New York 10010, U.S.A.
Penguin Books Australia Ltd, Ringwood, Victoria, Australia
Penguin Books Canada Ltd, 2801 John Street, Markham, Ontario, Canada L3R 1B4
Penguin Books (N.Z.) Ltd, 182–190 Wairau Road, Auckland 10, New Zealand

First published 1988

Grateful acknowledgement is made to the following for permission to reprint
previously published material:
Jonathan Cape for extracts from *The Second Sex* by Simone de Beauvoir,
English translation by H. M. Parshley, by permission of the estate of Simone
de Beauvoir.
William Collins Sons and Co. Ltd for extracts from *The Mandarins* by Simone
de Beauvoir © 1954 by Editions Gallimard, English translation copyright ©
1957 by Leonard Friedman.
André Deutsch for extracts from *Memoirs of a Dutiful Daughter, Prime of Life,
Force of Circumstance, All Said and Done, Old Age* and *A Very Easy Death* by
Simone de Beauvoir.
Editions Gallimard for extracts from *Simone de Beauvoir*, screenplay of a film
directed by Josée Dayan, © 1979 by Editions Gallimard. Also for extracts
from *Pour Une Morale de L'Ambiguité* by Simone de Beauvoir, © 1947 by Editions
Gallimard.

Made and printed in Great Britain by
Richard Clay Ltd, Bungay, Suffolk
Filmset in Monophoto Photina

For John, Joshua and Katrina

LIST OF PLATES

Marching for abortion, Paris 1971 (Magnum)

At home, 1975 (Archive Centre Audiovisuel Simone de Beauvoir)

With Sartre at his flat, 1978 (Agence Rapho)

Comforted by her sister at the funeral of Jean-Paul Sartre, 1980 (Popperfoto)

Supported by Lanzmann (right) at Sartre's funeral (Magnum)

NOTES AND ACKNOWLEDGEMENTS

To create a *brief* portrait of the life and work of a woman who dedicated some 2000 pages to creating her own is something of an intractable proposition. I have tried to render the flavour of Simone de Beauvoir's singular life, her judiciousness, the vitality of her intellect, as well as to highlight certain aspects of her most important books. None of this can stand in for a reading of her work. It is to Beauvoir herself that I owe my first and foremost debt.

Others have helped along the way. Margaret Walters's insights on Beauvoir re-stimulated my interest in her some years back. Conversations with Ronald Hayman helped me formulate my ideas, as did reading the recent and often highly critical feminist studies of Beauvoir's work. Emma Tennant and Tony Lacey offered support and encouragement when it was sorely needed. Above all, John Forrester, by giving me time when it was lacking, by listening patiently to my (as well as the children's) endless harangues and by reading these pages with a critical eye made this book possible. I owe him more than thanks.

In keeping with French usage, and to avoid awkwardness, I refer to Simone de Beauvoir as 'Beauvoir', rather than 'de Beauvoir', when using her name.

1908 9 January	Simone Lucie Ernestine Marie Bertrand de Beauvoir is born to Françoise (Brasseur) de Beauvoir and Georges de Beauvoir.
1910	Birth of Simone's only sibling, Hélène, nicknamed Poupette.
1913	Starts school at the Catholic Cours Désir where she stays until she receives her *baccalauréat*.
1919	The family's dwindling finances necessitate a move to a cheaper flat at 71 rue de Rennes.
1922	Loses her faith in God and is struck by the fact that she is now 'condemned to death'.
1924	Completes the first stage of the *baccalauréat*.
1925–6	Completes the second stage of her final examinations in philosophy and mathematics.
1927	Completes her *licence* and obtains a certificate in philosophy.
1928	Begins her studies at the Sorbonne and the École Normale Supérieure for her postgraduate *agrégation* in philosophy.
1929	Passes the written part of the *agrégation*. In July she meets Jean-Paul Sartre at the École Normale. They prepare for the oral part of the examination together and achieve top results.

In November Sartre begins his military service.

Simone starts writing and teaching part-time.

1931   Simone is appointed to a teaching post in Marseilles; Sartre to one in Le Havre.

1932   Finishes her first (unpublished) novel and is appointed to a new post in Rouen.

1933   Visits London with Sartre. Beginning of the triangular relationship with Olga Kosakiewicz.

1934   Visits Sartre in Berlin.

1936   Begins teaching at the Lycée Molière in Paris and moves to the hotel Royal-Bretagne on the rue de la Gaîté.

1937   Two publishers reject Simone's *Quand prime le spirituel* (*When Things of the Spirit Come First*), which is published by one of them, Gallimard, forty years later.

Begins work on *L'Invitée* (*She Came to Stay*).

1938   Sartre's *Nausea* appears, dedicated to Simone 'the Beaver'.

1939   War is declared and Sartre is drafted into the army.

From 1 September Simone begins to keep a journal of which a part appears in *Force of Circumstance*.

1940   Simone flees Paris in the face of the Nazi Occupation, but soon returns. Sartre is interned in a German prisoner-of-war camp.

1941   Sartre returns to Paris. The Resistance group, 'Socialisme et Liberté', is formed.

In July, Simone's father dies.

1943   Existentialism is born. Simone writes *Pyrrhus and Cinéas*.

In August *She Came to Stay* is published. She completes *The Blood of Others* and begins her third novel, *All Men are Mortal*.

1944   Paris is liberated. Simone becomes a founding editor of *Les Temps Modernes*.

1945	September sees the publication of *The Blood of Others*.
	Simone's only play, *Les Bouches Inutiles*, is a failure and closes after some fifty performances.
1946	In November *All Men are Mortal* is published.
1947	'Pour une morale de l'ambiguité' ('The Ethics of Ambiguity') is published in *Les Temps Modernes*.
	From 27 January until 20 May Simone visits the United States. She meets Nelson Algren in February.
	She starts working on what will become *The Second Sex*.
1948	*America Day by Day* is published in July.
	Extracts from *The Second Sex* begin to appear in *Les Temps Modernes*.
1949	Nelson Algren visits Paris in June.
	The Second Sex appears in two volumes in June and November and provokes a heated response.
	Simone begins work on *The Mandarins*.
1950	In August she goes to the US and spends two months with Algren.
1951	The affair with Algren is over.
1952	Benign tumour is removed from Simone's breast.
	She begins relationship with Claude Lanzmann; they decide to live together.
1953	*The Second Sex* appears in the US.
	In the autumn, she finishes *The Mandarins*.
1954	*The Mandarins* is published in October and receives the coveted Prix Goncourt.
1955	With the money from the Prix Goncourt, Simone buys the flat in which she spends the rest of her life.
	Visits China with Sartre and spends a week in Moscow on the return trip.
	Privilèges appears.

1957   *The Long March* is published.
        Simone is active on behalf of Algerian liberation.
1958   Sartre's health begins to deteriorate.
        In October *Memoirs of a Dutiful Daughter* is published
        to excellent reviews.
        Simone and Lanzmann separate.
1959   Continues militancy on behalf of Algerian war of
        liberation.
        'Brigitte Bardot and the Lolita Syndrome' is
        published in *Esquire*.
        Simone writes a preface to a book on family
        planning.
1960   Visits Cuba with Sartre and meets Castro.
        Campaigns on behalf of an Algerian woman,
        Djamila Boupacha, tortured by the French.
        Visits Brazil with Sartre.
        The second volume of Beauvoir's autobiography, *The
        Prime of Life*, appears in November.
1961   Because of activities against colonial rule in Algeria,
        Sartre's life is threatened and his flat bombed. He
        and Simone move several times under false names
        to avoid further attacks.
1962   Simone's life is threatened on the day that the book
        on Djamila Boupacha appears. On 18 March, peace
        in Algeria is declared.
1963   Publication of *Force of Circumstance* in October.
        In November Simone's mother dies. She begins to
        write *A Very Easy Death* which is published in the
        autumn of 1964.
1964   Simone writes a preface to her friend Violette
        Leduc's *La Batarde*.
1965   Visits the Soviet Union again with Sartre.
        Simone suffers a car accident and breaks several
        ribs.
        She begins writing *Les Belles Images*.

1966   She travels to Moscow and in the autumn to Japan where she and Sartre are heralded by an enthusiastic public.

1967   Visits the Middle East.
Participates in the Bertrand Russell Tribunal of War Crimes in Vietnam.

1968   *The Woman Destroyed* is published.
During the May events, Sartre and Simone side with the students.

1970   *Old Age* is published.
Simone takes part in a women's liberation demonstration demanding rights to abortion and contraception.

1971   Signs the Manifesto of 343, admitting to having had an illegal abortion.

1972   Simone declares herself a feminist.
Marches in protest against crimes against women.
The final volume of her autobiography, *All Said and Done*, is published in September.
Takes part in a film portrait of Sartre: *Sartre par lui-même*, much of which is filmed in her flat.

1973   Under Simone's direction, *Les Temps Modernes* starts a new section which asks readers to report on sexist behaviour.

1974   Simone is named President of the French League of Women's Rights.

1975   Simone makes her first television appearance in France.
She is awarded the Jerusalem prize for writers who have promoted the freedom of the individual.
She provides the commentary for a film on old age.

1978   Film portrait of Simone de Beauvoir is made by Josée Dayan and Malka Ribowska.

1979   Publication of her first set of short stories, *When Things of the Spirit Come First*.

1980   Death of Jean-Paul Sartre on 15 April. Simone falls into a depression which can only be partly relieved by work.

1981   Publication of *Adieux: A Farewell to Sartre*.
Death of Nelson Algren.

1983   Publication of *Lettres au Castor et à quelques autres* (Letters to the Beaver and to several others), Simone's edition of Sartre's letters.

1984   Claude Chabrol's film of Simone's second novel, *The Blood of Others*, opens in Paris. Simone has no desire to see it.

1986   Simone de Beauvoir dies in Paris on 14 April.

ONE

The Dutiful Daughter

I knew a great deal about Simone de Beauvoir well before I had set eyes on a single one of her books. In the sixties, in the snowy Canadian vastness where I grew up, her name had taken on legendary proportions. I knew that she was that coveted being: an independent woman. More than that, I knew she was an accomplished writer, an intellectual who held the keys to Paris – that magical city across the waters, crucible of twentieth-century culture. I imagined her as a sophisticated thirty year old dressed in existentialist black (the colour was far more familiar to me than the philosophy), whiling the days and nights away in cafés and clubs, a pen and notebook always to hand. The life she inhabited seemed intensely desirable.

What gave this life its ultimate mythical flourish was Simone de Beauvoir's relationship with the famous philosopher, Jean-Paul Sartre. They were the Humphrey Bogart and Lauren Bacall of the intellectual world, partners in a gloriously modern love affair. Indissolubly united, bound by complete intellectual understanding, Jean-Paul Sartre and Simone de Beauvoir were yet unmarried and free to engage in any number of 'contingent' relationships. In the marriage-bound, anti-intellectual morality of suburban Canada, the attraction of this union was incomparable, particularly for a book-loving adolescent girl eager to establish a sense of difference.

The aura of romance which surrounded Simone de Beauvoir's exemplary life did not diminish as I began to read her. *The Second Sex* was the first of her books I made my way through and as I turned its numerous pages, the scales seemed to fall from my eyes. Here was a terrifyingly lucid account of woman's condition, *my* condition as other in a world where the norm, with all its overarching power, was male. I was seized by a wish to imitate Simone de Beauvoir. When, some years later, I came to do postgraduate work, the theme of femininity became the core of my thesis.

For the women of my generation, Simone de Beauvoir took on something of the aspect of an idealized mother. Refusing children of her own, she gave birth instead to a movement, the agenda of which was set out in *The Second Sex*. But daughters, as they come of age, must needs rebel and good mothers be transformed into bad. Initially, for me, it was simply a question of creating some breathing space. In Simone de Beauvoir's omnisciently rational world, in the authority and moral rigour of her formulations – each of which seemed to imply that all achievement was simply a question of individual will – there was no room for murky confusions, uncontrollable circumstance and the irrationality of daily living.

Then, too, in those early heady days of the women's movement, when so many of us were engaged in uncovering and championing the very fact of our otherness, Simone de Beauvoir's assumption in *The Second Sex* that the masculine is the absolute human type to which women should aspire seemed a capitulation. Why should we women have to give up our femininity and recreate ourselves in the image of enlightened masculinity, when it would be so much better to re-imagine our entire culture!

And then came the final blow. The distant idol had feet of all too human clay. In reading the volumes of Beauvoir's massive autobiography, it became clear that not only did she consider her relationship with Jean-Paul Sartre to be the greatest achievement of her life, not only did she deem him intellecutally superior to herself (all of which I might have forgiven), but in this lifelong relationship of equals, he, it turned out, was far more equal than her. It was he who engaged in countless affairs, she who responded only on a small number of occasions by engaging in longer-lasting passionate affairs of her own. Worse. Between the lines of the autobiography, it was shockingly evident that Beauvoir suffered deeply from jealousy. Yet this most apparently honest and lucid of women preferred to avoid the issue, to evade the exploration of any irrational upsurge and keep the image of a model life intact.

When I came to reread Simone de Beauvoir for the purposes of this book, ambivalence about her and the project was intensified by the fact that I was pregnant. To be writing a book just then about a woman who had studiously excised children from her world, who saw maternity as a crucial factor in woman's subjection, constituted a not inconsiderable irony. But I found as I read through her remarkable

3

œuvre, as well as the various recent books which criticized her for her élitism, her lack of the appropriate feminist credentials, the universalist intent of her pronouncements, that I had finally arrived at an age where I could accept Simone de Beauvoir both good and bad. More than that I was filled with admiration for her intelligence, honesty and energy. I was prepared to defend her.

Unlike so many writers, Simone de Beauvoir's life is as public as her works and as important in its resonance. Whilst Sartre constructed a philosophy around the idea that life should be a continually recreated project, Simone de Beauvoir's life became her teaching: it was itself an exemplary project. On the surface this should make her an easy subject for a biographical portrait. From fiction to essays to autobiography, Beauvoir's life is written into her work, while her work is distilled life. Inevitably in writing this book I find myself moving from one to the other with little noticeable shift. Yet strangely the task of biography here is far from simple. Simone is so present that she becomes elusive. Her life and her work grow all but indistinguishable: how is one to sift the constructed life that emerges from her writing from the experience of living? Is there a Simone de Beauvoir who is different from the public and composed face she so skilfully presented us with? I think there are traces of her, and, in a way, the pain and difficulties evidenced by this Simone whom Beauvoir attempts to underplay make the project of her life all the more formidable.

Gifted with an irrepressible and inexhaustible energy, Simone de Beauvoir had that rare kind of intelligence which allowed her to seem eternally young and grow more radical with time. In 1968, at the age of sixty, she and Sartre stood on street corners selling revolutionary newspapers. A few years later when she marched for abortion and for women's rights, she seemed to have vaulted over the generations and become a woman of my time.

Yet Simone de Beauvoir's formative experience belongs to an epoch whose moral and intellectual codes are not our own. It marked her indelibly with a sense of propriety, a formality of speech and demeanour, as well as with a faith in human possibility and in the value of writing. If we look at her from within her own historical moment, her limitations seem at once more comprehensible and the scope of her achievement, her ability to transmit across to other generations, all the more remarkable.

Simone de Beauvoir was born on 9 January 1908 in Montparnasse, the Paris district which was to be her home for all but five years of her long life. From the window of the modest family flat, above the soon to be famous Café de la Rotonde, the little Simone, already an inveterate observer of the human spectacle, looked out on the hurly-burly of a neighbourhood in transition. Village was being transformed into city. All around demolition crews competed with construction workers, while the streets echoed to the sounds of hawkers, streetcars, and troops of donkeys and goats bound for the grazing fields of the Luxembourg Gardens.

Simone's extended family belonged to the wealthy bourgeoisie. As such, certain moral and social codes prevailed. Girls, it was assumed, would grow up to marry and do so within their own class. They would remain chaste until married and would pass from obeying their parents to obeying their husbands without straying inappropriately beyond the circle of approved families. Servants, city residences and summers in the country – all this was a matter of course.

Simone's birth coincided with the decline of her family's fortunes. Her maternal grandfather, a wealthy and speculation-loving Verdun banker, was declared a bankrupt and arrested. The attendant scandal in those days of Victorian respectability was considerable and Simone's mother felt herself thoroughly dishonoured. Not only did she break with all her previous circle, but she felt guilty towards Simone's father for the remainder of her life: her marriage dowry was never paid.

Prior to this, Simone's mother, Françoise Brasseur, had already suffered two emotional setbacks. As Beauvoir points out in *A Very Easy Death*, the deeply moving book which marks her ultimate reconciliation with her mother, Françoise Brasseur had had an unhappy childhood. Her own mother had never been interested in her children, while her father had a marked preference for her younger sister. In return, Simone, elder daughter that she was, reaped the ambivalent reward of being the primary object of her mother's attentions and aspirations.

A further disappointment was to follow for Françoise Brasseur. The cousin she was all but engaged to, once the spectre of encroaching bankruptcy reared its head, turned his attentions elsewhere. Not surprisingly in psychoanalytic terms, Simone's adolescent ardour was directed at Jacques Champigneulle, the son of the very man who had 'dropped' her mother. Never, her grandfather was heard to declare, will a granddaughter of mine marry a Champigneulle.

Passionate, headstrong, Françoise Brasseur was then allied to Georges de Beauvoir, the younger son of a family of Parisian civil servants and minor aristocrats. Elegant, witty, charming, with the free and easy self-assurance of the rich and well-born, there is no doubt that Georges de Beauvoir had all the attributes for appealing to a young woman. As Beauvoir writes:

When she was with my father she came into flower. She loved him, she admired him, and there is not the slightest doubt that for ten years he made her entirely happy physically. He loved women; he had had many affairs; and . . . he thought that a young wife ought not to be treated with less ardour than a mistress.

But neither his talents nor his will led Georges de Beauvoir to the law courts for which his education had destined him. He loved literature, women and social life, and above all else, the theatre. If he had been born into a class which countenanced his becoming one, he would have become an actor. As it was, much of his energy went into organizing amateur theatricals or creating the part that he played in his own life. His sense of his own specialness, his conviction that his aristocratic status removed him from the bourgeois vulgarity of work and the need to pursue success, did little to ensure his young family's well-being. Half-way between the old aristocracy of the Saint-Germain and the bourgeoisie, he belonged in fact to neither. A passionate admirer of her father in her youth, Simone was to be profoundly affected by his social displacement and the problems it gave rise to.

Nevertheless, the first years of Simone's life were, according to her own testimony, blissfully happy. A voluble, precocious child, she learned to read at the age of three and enjoyed a boundless curiosity which the extended family was eager to satisfy. At the age of seven she composed her first literary works, *The Misfortunes of Marguerite* and a parody of her family, *La Famille Cornichon* (The Gherkin Family). Petted and pampered, living in a circle of maternal warmth and physical delight, fed books and attention, she early developed a sense of her own specialness, a favoured difference which would stand her in good stead throughout her life. Stubborn, almost too full of energy, the young Simone was prone to violent and sometimes inexplicable tantrums, but they did little to mar this perfect early childhood.

Neither did the birth of her sister, Hélène, nicknamed Poupette, do anything to disturb Simone's impetuous vitality. Indeed Poupette, two-and-a-half years younger, became Simone's devoted playmate, perhaps all the dearer to Simone because she knew herself to be the parental favourite, the one who had the larger room, who had come first and continued to do so in parental eyes. It was Simone who taught Poupette to read and together the girls created elaborate imaginative games. Simone couldn't imagine how anyone could possibly have a good time without a younger sister.

She, of course, took the lead in everything and particularly enjoyed playing teacher to her sister's pupil. This gave her a sense of real authority, never obtainable even with malleable adults, as well as a pride in her own efficiency:

When I started to change ignorance into knowledge, when I started to impress truths upon a virgin mind, I felt I was at last creating something real ... I was breaking away from the passivity of childhood and entering the great human circle in which everyone is useful to everyone else.

If Simone occasionally sounds a little too much like the insufferably earnest and bossy elder sister, Hélène de Beauvoir's own words indicate the happy consequences of this sisterly influence. In a filmed conversation with Beauvoir, she explains how Simone was the only member of the family who didn't treat her as a complete inferior, the only one who, by preferring her to other little girls, gave her a sense of self-esteem. Interestingly, in the games of make-believe the sisters enacted, although Simone worked out the scenario, it was most often Poupette who took on the dominant role. Simone preferred to play the doomed but heroic saint, martyred by a tyrannical Poupette, who with the vengeful cruelty of the little sister, once joyfully tore up the devout Simone's prayerbook.

Catholicism, with its panoply of saints and martyrs, its hierarchy of sins, coloured Simone's childhood. Her mother was a zealous believer and the girls attended mass with her and performed morning and evening devotions. The intimacy Simone shared with her pious mother led her not only to enjoy a brief desire to become a nun, but also confuse her all-seeing mother with God Himself. Such was Madame de Beauvoir's sense of maternal responsibility, that in 1913 when Simone was enrolled at that Catholic institution for young ladies, the Cours Adeline Désir, her mother went with her, knitted during classes and began to study Latin and English so as to monitor Simone's progress.

The fact that she attended a school again marked Simone's difference from her extended family and social peers. Most other young girls of her class were educated by governesses at home, but such expense was beyond the means of the Beauvoirs. Simone, however, loved the world of school and felt herself fortunate. Learning was a never ending adventure, the work itself boundless pleasure and when her mother first took her to a library, this 'paradise of abundance', she experienced one of the greatest joys of her childhood.

If Simone's mother and father agreed with one another on the importance of education and literary culture for their children, on questions of faith they were radically opposed. Georges de Beauvoir was a non-believer and he often aired his scepticism on religious matters. Yet Simone never heard her parents argue on the subject. She was so deeply imbued with the idea of God, that she was initially content calmly to accept what was later to become an intolerable contradiction. 'I grew accustomed to the idea,' she writes in *Memoirs of a Dutiful Daughter*, 'that my intellectual life – embodied by my father – and my spiritual life – expressed by my mother – were two radically heterogeneous fields of experience which had nothing in common. Sanctity and intelligence belonged to two quite different spheres; and human things – culture, politics, business, manners, and customs – had nothing to do with religion.'

Although Simone's father may have been a free-thinker in matters of religion, his political sympathies were for the extreme right wing. He was opposed not only to universal suffrage, but also, because of his aristocratic pretensions, to the Republic. Particularly during and after the 1914–18 War, his diatribes against socialism and internationalism, but especially against those supposed foreigners who were bringing down French civilization from within, grew increasingly fervent.

The war itself was less unkind to the Beauvoir family than to many others. A first flush of patriotic enthusiasm saw a dutiful Simone excelling herself in making flags and banners, while a delighted Georges de Beauvoir donned the theatrical garb of a Zouave regiment. A heart attack sent him home some three months later. He then devoted his time to creating spectacles for soldiers and to shaping the literary tastes of his children. The family had never been so close. Every evening Georges de Beauvoir read to a delighted threesome from the French classics – Racine, Corneille, Molière, Edmond Rostand and Victor Hugo. He created a notebook anthology for Simone's own use and had her do difficult dictations. He sang for them, acted, did imitations and Simone's admiration for him burgeoned.

But the family's financial means declined. Nothing, not a piece of string, not a crust of bread was ever wasted. At one point, Simone was so imbued with a sense of economy that she began to cram her school notebooks with the most miniscule of scripts. The teachers complained to her mother, but the principle of 'no waste' stayed with Simone throughout her life. 'I remained convinced that one must make use of everything, and of one's self, to the utmost.'

In 1919 the Beauvoirs were forced to move to a fifth-floor flat in the Rue de Rennes. Dank and dirty, the building had no lift or running water. Simone and Poupette shared a room and only the study, where Simone often worked at her father's desk, had a wood fire. The drudgery of maintaining this household without a servant – something quite unheard of in bourgeois circles – transformed Françoise de Beauvoir from a beautiful woman into a harassed and perpetually worried one. She pushed her new neglect and contempt of the body so far that it affected the girls' cleanliness. Their clothes were always hand-me-downs, threadbare from overuse, their hair matted. In her first stories, only to be published in the seventies, as well as in her memoirs, Simone de Beauvoir records her shame at her ill-fitting dresses, how they only accentuated her clumsiness, and how badly the sisters' dull attire, their dirty nails and torn stockings, compared to that of their rich friends and relatives.

Yet family attitudes turned necessity into virtue. The girls were taught that culture and piety were far more important than riches. Despite their poverty, Simone was made to feel that she was 'one in a million' and entitled to consider her taste for reading and her scholastic successes as tokens of personal superiority which would ensure her future destiny. This cluster of values – a sense of puritanism, a disdain for the material surfaces of life, a belief that salvation lay in the intellect – was to separate Simone off from the majority of her circle and to stay with her throughout her life.

Needless to say, the Beauvoirs' continuing poverty also had its very real ill effects. Georges de Beauvoir, after a further speculative fiasco dreamt up by his irrepressible father-in-law, found work through the intervention of a relative as an advertising salesman for a newspaper. As his youthful aspirations to an aristocratic life vanished and bitterness set in, his behaviour changed. The charming, gallant man was no more. Instead, Georges de Beauvoir began to outdo the poor he now materially belonged to by imitating what he conceived of as their 'vulgar' manners. In public he would talk in a booming voice and hurl abuse at strangers in an accent not his own. At home, he derided everything and everyone. Increasingly, as Simone grew into her teens, he would spend the nights out, frequenting brothels, coming home in the morning reeking of drink and concocting tales of all-night card games.

Françoise de Beauvoir continued to play the dutiful wife, but her temper deteriorated. As Simone de Beauvoir recounts in *A Very Easy Death*, there were 'slaps, nagging, scenes, not only in privacy, but even when guests were present'.

It is impossible for anyone to say 'I am sacrificing myself' without feeling bitterness. One of Maman's contradictions was that she thoroughly believed in the nobility of devotion, while at the same time she had tastes, aversions and desires that were too masterful for her not to loathe whatever went against them. She was continually rebelling against the restraints and the privations that she inflicted upon herself.

It was just as her daughters were coming to an age when they wanted more freedom, more solitude, that Madame de Beauvoir began increasingly to need them as a compensation for the deprivations in her own life. She grew overbearing, possessive, determined to have her daughters in her power. Already at the early and obedient age of eight, Simone had learned that it was best to keep certain things from her mother – 'a curious itching sensation between my

13

legs', anything to do with the 'fruit of thy womb' or 'ties of blood' – all this was forbidden territory. It was not proper to talk of bodily things; indeed, 'I learnt that my body as a whole was vulgar and offensive'. Books too, the young Simone discovered, delved into these improper matters. Madame de Beauvoir, who carefully monitored her children's reading, would pin together pages inappropriate for their eyes.

For many years Simone did not dream of transgressing these imposed limits, but her curiosity persisted and her mother's anxious prudery only served to charge the unknown with a dangerous fascination. Priestly prohibitions similarly stimulated her inquisitiveness and presented the ever logical Simone with an insoluble conundrum. How could knowledge of what adults seemed to agree existed in reality lead to despair and damnation, prove fatal simply because one was too young or unmarried? The sisters sought answers from their elder cousin, Madeleine, one summer in the country, where their freedom was always greater. Madeleine was allowed to read what she liked, but her explanations served only to confuse them. When Poupette, less inhibited than Simone, confronted their mother on their return, Madame de Beauvoir led them to believe that babies came out of the anus, quite painlessly. 'I never again discussed these problems with her,' Simone de Beauvoir writes, 'and she never said another word to us about them.' Disillusionment with the superiority of adults began to set in.

With adolescence it took full wing and Simone became increasingly irritated by her own habit of obedience. She met her mother's demands with increasing reticence and was resentful of the fact that she was controlled by a woman whose views she had begun to find ridiculous. Moreover, she grew jealous of the hold her mother had on her father's affections, despite their differences in outlook. This was exacerbated by the fact that her father was now disappointed in her, critical of her adolescent unattractiveness, and preferred her pretty, younger sister. Simone's attempts to s' ength-then her intellectual intimacy with her father only resulted in her parents putting on a united front, imposing duti-fulness on her in the face of common sense. Simone's reaction was to grow secretive, merely to pretend compliance. Her rebellion had begun: forbidden books were now her everyday reading and she gained a somewhat less hazy notion of sexual relations. She also started to question the place of religion in the world, which set an even greater distance between her mother and herself. This rejection of everything that her mother stood for was to colour her understanding of the world well into her middle life.

As she points out in *Memoirs of a Dutiful Daughter*, Simone de Beauvoir was brought up with a conventional set of bourgeois values which was at once 'monolithic and incoherent'. These values permitted her mother's convent morality to coexist with her father's nationalism: 'Neither my mother nor my teachers doubted for a moment that the Pope was elected by the Holy Spirit; yet my father thought His Holiness should not interfere in world affairs and my mother agreed with him.' National values came before Catholic virtues and Caesar always got the better of God.

Simone's breach with faith came appropriately at Meyrig-nac in the Limousin, her paternal grandfather's country estate, where Simone spent her summers. It was here that she learned that love of nature which was never to leave her. In the country, for the young Simone, there was no poverty and less parental supervision. Simone spent many joyful monents in solitary communion with sky and trees and fields which for her were the very emanation of a divine presence. But then something changed. The fourteen-year-old Simone had been pondering why it was that the truth about religion should be *women's* privilege, when men, beyond all possible doubt, were their superiors. Leaning out of the window of her room one night, she was suddenly aware of an absence in heaven and in her heart. All day long she had been indulging in forbidden activities, deliberate disobediences. If she had believed in God, she realized, she could not so easily have behaved sinfully, allowed herself to offend Him. She loved the world more than the God whom she had refined into oblivion, and now, conscious of this, she was too much of an extremist to compromise. Simone made a clean break.

Visible in this rupture with faith is the intellectual rigour which characterizes Beauvoir's approach to life as a whole. She will allow for murkiness, for what she calls 'humbug' neither in herself, nor in others. Yet her stringent lucidity often carries pain in its wake. The young Simone was devastated by this new 'emptiness of heaven'. She was desolate, 'Alone: without a witness, without anyone to speak to, without refuge'. Even more terrifying was the realization that she was now condemned to death. Despair overwhelmed her – an annihilating fear which was to haunt her throughout her adult life and which she kept at bay by her optimistic dedication to energetic activity.

Simone did not tell her mother of her lapse from faith. Out of respect, she continued for some time to act out a life of obedience.'Everything was as before: the concept of duty, righteousness, sexual taboos.' But she lived a double life where there was no relationship between her inner self and the self that others saw. This disjuncture, in the conservative circles in which she moved, was a lonely and painful one.

As soon as the young Simone had given up hopes of heaven, her worldly ambitions increased. She had long ago decided to devote herself to intellectual work and rejected the maternal model. At the age of fifteen, she unhesitatingly answered the question 'What do you want to do later in life?' with 'To be a famous author'. Her father rated writers higher than philosophers, scholars or professors, and Simone was also convinced of their supremacy. Literature would guarantee her the immortality she had lost with her faith in heaven. It would also allow her to serve humanity.

'Simone has a man's brain. She thinks like a man,' Georges de Beauvoir had always said. But paradoxically, as Simone's scholastic brilliance persisted and saw her through the Cours Désir to the academically sounder Institut Sainte-Marie and the various nationwide competitive examinations in philosophy, mathematics and literature, her father began to bemoan the fact that he had raised a bluestocking. Her very success, her ability to pursue a career and make a living was a testimony to his own failure. 'The daughters of his friends, his brothers and his sisters would be "ladies", but not me.'

As Beauvoir explains in the *Memoirs*:

In those days people of my parent's class thought it unseemly for a young lady to go in for higher education – to train for a profession was a sign of defeat . . . He was of the opinion that to shine in those exalted spheres [of high society] a woman should not only be beautiful and elegant but should also be well read and a good conversationalist; so he was pleased with my early scholastic successes . . . But though my father liked intelligent and witty women, he had no time for bluestockings. When he announced, 'My dears, you'll never marry. You'll have to work for your living', there was bitterness in his voice

Georges de Beauvoir also thought teachers were low-minded pedagogues and he mourned the fact that Simone had decided on this profession. It would make her an intellectual, place her in the ranks of those who applauded the Rights of Man, pacifism, internationalism and socialism. The best he could hope for from his daughter was that she would become an intellectual prodigy – a phenomenon who would accumulate diplomas and be seen as someone not to be judged by normal standards.

Confused by her father's evident dissatisfaction with her, despite the fact that she seemed to be fulfilling all his wishes, Simone was unhappy and ill at ease. Her gradual resentment combined with her growing scepticism to allow her, far later than was the case with her mother, to reject her father's values, and rebel wholeheartedly against her family.

What Simone de Beauvoir garnered from her early family life was an ingrained sense that power, the intellectual life and the potential for shaping one's own destiny were the property of the male. The married woman, on the other hand, occupied a wholly unenviable position: one in which she had to succumb to male authority and inevitably become a martyr to her children. Only a grim tenacity – which she came to respect later in life, once her own rebellion had been accomplished – allowed her mother to maintain her own beliefs in the face of male authority. The costs, in accommodation, in suppressed rage, in a deformation of character, were high. From very early in life, Simone identified with the male. She vowed never to marry and her family's restricted circumstances ensured that no appropriate man would present himself. By choice and by contingency, she was destined for a career.

This was not the case for her closest childhood friend, Elizabeth Mabille, known in the memoirs as Zaza. Zaza, whom Simone met at the Cours Désir at the age of ten, was the daughter of a wealthy Catholic family who, unlike Simone's parents, were involved in public life and in the democratic wing of Catholic activity. Far more sophisticated than the bookish Simone, fearless in her criticisms of everything and everyone, Zaza became the object of Simone's childhood longings, her first friend as well as her first love – though Zaza herself was unaware of Simone's idolatry until they were both at university.

Together the girls attended the Institut Sainte-Marie where Simone became infatuated with Robert Garric, the founder of a movement of social welfare groups, destined to bring students together with workers and forge progress through friendship beyond class divisions. Simone was so moved by Garric's polemics that she vowed her life to the service of humanity, as she had before, in her moments of youthful mysticism. vowed herself to the service of God.

Every moment of her time was scrupulously used and she abjured all frivolous reading matter, resenting the time it took to brush her teeth, clean her nails, or engage in the polite conversation her family demanded of her. At meals Simone would be studying Greek, at other times preparing for the papers in literature, taught by Garric, or in philosophy, mathematics, and classics. She became a monster of insensitivity, speaking only to voice vigorous disgust at her father's conservative literary tastes or his traditional ideas about women and marriage. But she did make time for Garric's groups – only to find them a total disappointment. Friendships between the classes were not to be forged by woolly rhetoric and inspired illusions.

Zaza had always had reservations about Robert Garric and had not been overtaken by Simone's fanatical zeal. There were other differences between them. Unlike Simone, Zaza still took part in the expansive social life of her family and took on the household chores demanded of her. This prevented her from throwing herself fully into university life and, quite often, from seeing Simone. Her deep attachment to her mother made real rebellion against the expectations she had of her impossible. Her year of further education was merely a respite: the fate of marriage to a man of her parents' choice awaited her. Simone reproached her with defeatism. Her own buoyant optimism, her determination, left her with little patience for Zaza's growing apathy and despair.

Some three years after their shared year at the Institut Sainte-Marie, Zaza succumbed to meningitis and died, victim of a conflict between her loyalty to her mother and her love for the philosopher Maurice Merleau-Ponty (known in the

Memoirs as Jean Pradelle) to whom Simone had introduced her. Her family's disapproval of Merleau-Ponty seemed incomprehensible to both Zaza and Simone: he was Catholic, came of an apparently good family. So did Merleau-Ponty's own refusal to press his case for Zaza's hand.

It has since been revealed that the Mabilles' refusal to permit the alliance between Merleau-Ponty and Zaza came from their secret knowledge that Merleau-Ponty was illegitimate, the son of an adulterous liaison. For the Catholic Mabilles, adultery was a mortal sin and an alliance between Zaza and Merleau-Ponty unthinkable. Unwilling to destroy his own sister's forthcoming marriage if news of his mother's adultery made the rounds, Merleau-Ponty told Monsieur Mabille that he would withdraw his suit. Zaza, ignorant of all this, was so distressed by Merleau-Ponty's sudden coolness, that her mother finally explained the circumstances to her. Unable to cope with the destruction of her love, unable to disobey her parents, Zaza slipped into madness and succumbed to fever. Too late, her parents were willing to withdraw their prohibition.

For Simone, Zaza's tragic death represented a clear case of victimization by an oppressive bourgeois morality. Zaza's fate could so easily have been hers that, years later, she still believed that her friend had paid for Simone's freedom with her own death. Zaza's story and what it revealed about the suffocating values of her own class was to haunt all of Simone's early attempts at fiction.

One other love featured in Simone's young life. Throughout her teens, she nursed an infatuation for her cousin, Jacques Champigneulle, whom she had known since childhood. Handsome, free from parental constraints, Jacques had an artistic bent and vowed to turn his family's stained glass firm into a concern which produced objects of artistic beauty. It was he who introduced Simone to the contemporary French literature her father so vociferously condemned; he, too, who spent his nights in the bars and clubs frequented by the artistic avant-garde and prohibited to Simone. She romanticized his image, saw in him what she herself wished to become – that agonized inhabitant of a Bohemia made popular by the literature of the day. With parental encouragement, she transformed this rare male friendship into a relationship which had a fantasized future in marriage. Simone herself was never certain she wanted the marriage. But Jacques, during her lonely years of early adolescent rebellion, was the only man she could talk problems over with, the only friend who seemed to share her own discomfort with their background. 'His blasé, sulky face, his evasive eyes, the books he had lent me, his half-confidences – everything convinced me that he lived with his face turned towards an uncertain future ... I saw in Jacques the perfect incarnation of disquiet.'

Yet Jacques never proposed, never even kissed her – though this lack of a sexual approach seemed all but insignificant to a Simone who still lived within the aura of familial prudery. As her range of friendships grew with her university years, she found that her relationship with Jacques swung from near indifference when he was present and attentive, or even mild contempt at his constant negativity, to wild longing, jealousy and marital day-dreams when he was away.

The day-dreams ended when Simone suddenly learned that Jacques was to be married to the daughter of a wealthy family who could provide a substantial dowry. As his father before him had done to Simone's mother, Jacques abandoned Simone. The hero of her youth had been transformed into a 'calculating bourgeois'.

It could be said that, in Jacques, Simone had found a male version of herself – the boy she might have been had her mother married her first love. In falling in love with him, Simone was unconsciously following the path her mother had trodden before her. In so doing, she may well have been hoping to succeed where her mother had failed. Such a love affair might be construed as an aggressive act of transgresssion, an invasion of maternal territory: in effect an act of *lèse-majesté*. But at the same time, it was also a magnanimous act of reparation: Simone was making good the loss that she herself, the girl child of a marriage to someone who was not a Champigneulle, represented – namely the loss of Jacques Champigneulle's father. Through this dreamed-of marriage, her mother would at last have a male Champigneulle.

The fact that the mercenary considerations of both Champigneulles, father and son, ruled the destinies of both Françoise and Simone could not but have had an effect on a dutiful daughter's appreciation of bourgeois marriage. In later life, it may not just have been Sartre's desire for freedom that decided Simone never to marry; she certainly had her own reasons for eschewing the institution. And it may not be coincidental that, after waking from the dream of marriage to Jacques, her mother no longer figures significantly in the life Simone recounts, until the 'very easy death' reactivates the earlier identification. After Jacques Champigneulle, Simone was never to dream of marriage so concretely again.

She did however attempt to experience that 'hazardous and useless' existence whose attractions Jacques and the younger novelists were always praising. Having been introduced to the adventure of cafés and bars by Jacques, Simone, sometimes accompanied by her sister, would occasionally find a pretext to escape from her mother's vigilant eye and have a night on the town. She would sit on her bar stool in the fashionable Jockey Club and, with all the fervour which had formerly made her kneel before the Holy Sacrament, she would inhale tobacco fumes and drink. She would behave outlandishly, exchange loud insults and slaps with a supposedly unknown Poupette, pretend to be a model or a prostitute, though with her dingy clothes, sensible shoes and face free of make-up, she suspected, in retrospect, that she never deceived anyone. In her defiance of convention and authority, she would dance with strangers, enjoying the sensation of unknown hands caressing her. Eventually, too, in accordance with the edicts of her new literary masters – such as André Gide and Jacques Rivière – to live dangerously and perform gratuitous acts, Simone would allow herself to be accosted in the streets and spend evenings drinking with strange men.

Though Beauvoir never mentions this in her memoirs, there is something in her portrayal of her rebellious behaviour during her late teens which suggests that she was at once modelling herself on her father and trying to outdo him in impermissible acts. Simone has the brain of a man, he had said often enough. In her embrace of the dangerous, in her forays into low life, in coming home in the early hours and affirming implausible alibis, she was also proving that she had the freedom to *act* like a man, albeit the trivial freedom of the bourgeois man.

Yet Simone was still subject to a prudery which made sexuality repugnant to her. The thought of lust, unredeemed by love, the slightest allusion to fleshly things, caused her an indescribable distress. It was equivalent to a fall from grace:

Obviously I did not hold that one should languish in perpetual virginity. But I was sure the wedding night should be a white mass: true love sublimates the physical embrace, and in the arms of her chosen one the pure young girl is briskly changed into a radiant young woman.

Whatever the force of her rebellion against her mother's faith, Simone kept its structures intact and for many years to come thought in terms of a secular and perhaps romantic salvation.

TWO

A Necessary Love

In 1927 Simone de Beauvoir completed her degree in literature and philosophy at the Sorbonne University in Paris.
The following year she began her work for the postgraduate
'*agrégation*' –a professional teaching qualification – in part
at the élite École Normale Supérieure. Her brilliance as a
student is uncontested; the friendships, so lacking in childhood, now burgeon. She has a reputation for trenchant
intellect; and her bold opinions, delivered rapidly and forcefully in a brusque voice provide a striking contrast to her
elegant manners and demeanour.

It was at the Lycée Janson de Sailly that Simone undertook
her teaching practice. Her co-students included the philosopher Maurice Merleau-Ponty and the founder of structural
anthropology, Claude Lévi-Strauss. As the first woman ever
to teach philosophy in a boys' *lycée*, the uniqueness of
Simone's position seemed a natural progression from the
special place she had always felt she occupied as a child. Her
male colleagues, she was later to write, treated her with an
exceptional kindness, lacking in any condescension.

Their friendliness prevented me from ever taking up that challenging attitude which later was to cause me so much dismay when I encountered it in American women: from the start men were my comrades, not my enemies. Far from envying them, I felt that my own position, from the very fact that it was an unusual one, was one of privilege.

It was only in the 1970s that Beauvoir would see the contradictions in this position and understand the workings of tokenism. During most of her life, individual intellectual and literary achievement served as a pass-key into the freedom of the male world she valued far above the constricted world of women.

Among the École Normale students enrolled for the prestigious *agrégation* in philosophy, one small group had gained a certain notoriety for their unchallenged superiority and audacious antics. The group included Paul Nizan, already a published author and member of the Communist Party, René Maheu (known in the memoirs as André Herbaud) and Jean-Paul Sartre. At an end-of-year party at the École Normale, Sartre had appeared nude in a satirical sketch and created a scandal which reverberated through the school's élite walls for many years.

Simone struck up a friendship with Maheu, a married man with literary aspirations. It was he who gave her the long-lasting nickname, Castor or Beaver (the supposed English pronunciation for Beauvoir), because, he claimed, 'Beavers like company and have a constructive bent'. It was also he who introduced Castor to Jean-Paul Sartre, though he was anxious that Simone should not allow Sartre to replace him in her affections.

27

Simone was working on a thesis on the eighteenth-century philosopher Leibniz and, through Maheu, Sartre sent her a drawing which represented Leibniz bathing with the Monads. He wanted to meet her and suggested a date. Afraid that Sartre would take advantage of his absence, Maheu asked Simone not to go. She sent her sister, Poupette, in her place, explaining that she had had to leave suddenly for the country. Sartre's and Simone's meeting was delayed until the time of the final examinations in July 1929. Following on the written part, there would be an oral. Sartre and Nizan invited Simone to revise with them.

Simone de Beauvoir describes her awe on her first encounter with this circle of the elect:

Sartre greeted me in a worldly manner; he was smoking a pipe. Nizan, who said nothing, had a cigarette stuck in the corner of his one-sided smile and was quizzing me through his pebble lenses, with an air of thinking more than he cared to say. All day long, petrified with fear, I annotated the 'metaphysical treatise' . . .

Soon she relaxed, but she still had to rack her brains to find arguments to put to the loquacious and seemingly omniscient Sartre. His intellectual range, his generosity as a teacher, staggered her, as did the irreverence of the entire group's attitudes.

When they were all together the three 'comrades' didn't pull their punches. Their language was aggressive, their thought categorical, their judgments merciless. They made fun of bourgeois law and order; they had refused to sit the examination in religious knowledge: I had no difficulty in agreeing with them on that score. But I was still, in many respects, the dupe of bourgeois humbug; *they* jabbed a pin in every inflated idealism, laughed high-minded souls to scorn – in fact, every kind of soulfulness, the 'inner life', the marvellous, the mysterious, and the precious all fell under their lashing contempt; on every possible occasion – in their speech, their attitudes, their gestures, their jokes – they set out to prove that men were not rarefied spirits but bodies of flesh and bone, racked by physical need and crudely engaged in a brutal adventure that was life.

The still soulful and intellectually respectful Simone, who could lose herself in the wonders of nature, was shocked. But she recognized that here, at last, she was in touch with people who weren't afraid to look reality in the face, to be irreverent and question conventional assumptions, whether philosophical or social, with a vehement rigour. It was something she had always longed to do. At last she felt she belonged.

In the days leading up to the examination, Sartre and Simone never left each other except to sleep. They talked ceaselessly and about everything. Simone had never met anyone whose knowledge was so deep and so wide: 'The freshness and dogged tenacity of his perceptions grasped the very essence of things in all their lively profusion. How cramped my little world seemed beside this exuberantly abundant universe!' Sartre also made it clear that he was interested in *her* and when he analysed Simone with the passionate energy he put into all thought, it was not from his own point of view, but as a genuine attempt to understand her in the light of her own values and attitudes. What could be more appealing to a young woman who had always felt cut off from her circle and who valued intellectual endeavour above anything else? The crowning touch, for

Simone, came when she realized that Sartre shared her literary aspirations. Yet here he was miles ahead of her. 'I had thought I was an exceptional person because I couldn't imagine living and not writing: but he lived only in order to write.' For the first time in her life Simone felt intellectually inferior to another person. Sartre's culture was much wider and more firmly grounded than hers. It included a knowledge of popular films and books, westerns and thrillers, which Simone, with her love of 'high art' altogether ignored. Moreover Sartre already had a precise idea of the kinds of books he wanted to write, whereas she had gone on, as she herself states, 'fatuously declaring that I "would tell all"; it was at once too much and too little'.

The twosome read each other's work and that process of frank criticism, that dialogue about each other's literary production which was to last throughout their shared life, was set in motion. In the examination for the *agrégation*, Sartre came first, though the examiners, recognizing that Sartre had already sat and failed the exam once before, hesitated for a long time over the final outcome of the ranking. They were agreed that despite Sartre's evident qualities, intelligence and culture, the *real* philosopher was Simone de Beauvoir.

From Simone's point of view there was never any doubt. Despite the fact that at twenty-one, she was the youngest person ever in France to pass this highly competitive examination, Sartre was distinctly her superior. Simone de Beauvoir was in love: 'Sartre corresponded exactly to the dream companion I had longed for since I was fifteen: he was the double in whom I found all my burning aspiration raised to the pitch of incandescence. I should always be able to share everything with him.'

Who was this young man who answered so perfectly to Simone's dreams? Born two-and-a-half years before Simone on the other side of Paris, Jean-Paul Satre was brought up for the first eleven years of his life by an idolizing mother and a grandfather, Charles Schweitzer, whose intellectual vigour and love of women were certainly traits he passed onto his grandson. Jean-Paul's father died when he was a little over one and his mother moved back to her own parental home which Charles Schweitzer – a leading peda-gogue and teacher of English and German – ran with un-disputed authority. Charles Schweitzer took over the young Jean-Paul's education. The Alsatian Schweitzers were bil-ingual and Sartre was brought up speaking both French and German. Very early he started to write stories, put the *Fables* of La Fontaine into verse and by the age of ten, he was corresponding with his grandfather in alexandrines.

When his mother remarried an engineer who ran the naval works in La Rochelle, Jean-Paul was desolate. Anne-Marie Sartre had been the young Sartre's ardent and close companion, accompanying him on daily walks to the Luxem-bourg Gardens, on frequent visits to the theatre, circus and especially the cinema, and initiating him into the world of music, which was to remain a life-long love.

The young Sartre hated his step-father, an intruder on Oedipal intimacy. In the La Rochelle secondary school he was sent to, he was viewed as a Parisian prig by his rough and ready peers. Sartre learned to use his fists, stole money from his mother to buy his classmates treats and win them over. A constant fantasist and scribbler, aware from an early age, like Simone, of his specialness, he penned long heroic adventures for himself. Sent back to Paris to the famous Lycée Henri IV to terminate his secondary education and compete for the *grandes écoles*, Sartre forged a reputation for himself not only for intellectual brio, but for scabrous wit. With his closest friend, Paul Nizan, he constructed and performed satirical sketches in which the world, as well as teachers and friends, were put on trial. By the time he met Simone de Beauvoir, he had already broached some of the points of the philosophical system which was to become known as existentialism.

Small, wall-eyed, Sartre made up for his physical unattractiveness by the sheer force of his exuberant personality and charm. He knew how to listen, how to please and how to entertain. When he met Simone, he had already broken off one marital engagement and was a youth of some sexual experience. He saw himself as a Don Juan, a seducer who ruptured conventions and whose presence revealed things in their essence. Seduction and writing, he believed, had their source in the same intellectual process. In a 1976 interview he admitted that he imagined a succession of women for himself, each one meaning everything for a given moment. It was Simone's qualities which resulted in her taking on a unique place in his life. 'We understood what we meant to one another,' he said. Yet Sartre's initial reaction to this serious, blue-eyed philosophy student did not smack of love at first sight. 'Engaging, pretty, but badly dressed,' he commented to his friends. The relationship blossomed quickly, however, and after the summer holidays during which Sartre visited Simone in the Limousin and letters flew back and forth, it took on a deeper note.

In the opening pages of the second volume of her autobiography, *The Prime of Life*, Beauvoir describes her joy at moving out of her parent's house into a room of her own in her maternal grandmother's flat in Montparnasse. Her grandmother rented out rooms and treated Simone with the same respect as her other tenants. With all the excitement of a woman creating for the first time a secret den from which prying eyes can at last be kept at bay, Simone papers her walls in a bright orange, gathers together bits and pieces of furniture – a table, a chair, a divan, bookshelves. She finds part-time teaching work at a *lycée* and supplements her income with private tutoring. After the years of dreary clothes and heavy-duty fabrics, she splurges and buys herself crêpe de Chine and velvety garments and totally impractical high-heeled slippers which she wears at all times, despite their unsuitability for the classrooms of a *lycée*. She dabs on make-up, powder, rouge and liberal quantities of lipstick. She is, at last, an independent woman. But as she says, 'My new life really began when Sartre returned to Paris in mid-October.'

If Simone were a writer of the 1970s engaged on a confessional literary voyage we might have had a full-blown description of her and Sartre's initial sexual encounter, her loss of virginity and so on. As it is, Beauvoir maintains a near Victorian muteness about the sexual side of her and Sartre's relationship. 'I had surrendered my virginity with glad abandon: when heart, head, and body are all in unison, there is high delight to be had from the physical expression of that oneness.' This said, it is the rational, the intellectual side of their union to which she gives precedence – Sartre and her shared aspirations and mutual projects.

From our present vantage point it is difficult fully to appreciate the sheer adventurousness and unconventionality of the pact which Simone de Beauvoir and Sartre forged. Particularly from Simone's side, the woman's side, the break from accepted norms was monumental, as was the social stigma it bore. Lovers, Sartre and Simone were yet not to be married, even though they foresaw a lasting relationship. Sartre did not believe in monogamy. It was too stultifying a state for a writer who fed off the new, who needed a wide range of experience and emotions to nurture his work. This did not shock Simone. Sartre was only repeating what, from her father's example and bourgeois practices, she knew to be a male prerogative, though he had the honesty to voice his intentions openly. What was different in the way that Sartre outlined their future union was that she, the woman, was to be equally free and would also engage in outside relationships.

'What *we* have,' he said to Simone, 'is an *essential* love; but it is a good idea for us also to experience *contingent* love affairs.' By contingent Sartre meant that which could alter, that which is important but not of primary importance. Beauvoir writes, recording Sartre's proposal: 'We were two of a kind, and our relationship would endure as long as we did: but it could not make up entirely for the fleeting riches to be had from encounters with different people.'

Simone agreed. The proposition suited her own ideas, her dissatisfaction with what she had witnessed of conventional marriage. She agreed, too, to Sartre's dictum of 'transparency' – the vow that they would never lie to one another as married couples did. Rather they would tell each other everything and share their feelings, their work, their projects.

For Sartre, this pact allowed him to maintain his taste for seduction, for travel and adventure and allayed his fear of being tied down, swallowed up by a woman. For Simone, although rationally she welcomed the contours of the proposal and felt in all good faith that it was what she wanted – a strategy which would suit her desire to be independent and a writer – matters were far more difficult. As a woman in the 1920s she could hardly engage with the same ease as Sartre in haphazard sexual encounters. Nor, even if social mores permitted, would her puritan formation have made it a simple matter for her to do so. In one of the few passages in her autobiography where Beauvoir discusses her sexuality, this becomes clear.

The relationship with Sartre had woken Simone's physical side, but given the prudery of her upbringing, this is a mixed blessing. She is shocked by the strength of the sensuality released in her, overwhelmed by the recognition of the sheer force of simple physical desire. During Sartre's numerous absences, her body is prey to irrepressible whims she cannot control. She finds the split between conscious will and violent physical emotions alarming in the extreme:

From the roots of my hair to the soles of my feet a poisoned shirt was woven over my body . . . Starved of its sustenance [my body] begged and pleaded with me; I found it repulsive. I was forced to admit a truth that I had done my best to conceal ever since adolescence: my physical appetites were greater than I wanted them to be. In the feverish caresses and love-making that bound me to the man of my choice I could discern the movements of my heart, my freedom as an individual. But that mood of solitary, languorous excitement cried out for anyone, regardless.

For Simone, passion within the bounds of love is acceptable, but the discovery that when the body calls any man will do is shattering. She can neither easily satisfy these tyrannical desires, nor, more importantly, can she confess their existence to Sartre, to whom she had vowed to tell all.

If I dared not confess such things, it was because they were by definition unavowable. By driving me into such secrecy my body became a stumbling block rather than a bond of union between us, and I felt a burning resentment against it.

It is interesting to note that in one of her very last interviews Beauvoir says that in her case, her head has always been far stronger than her body, her desires. This particular passage, this episode in her life, would however suggest that a real battle between the two did nonetheless exist, and in the service of her relationship with Sartre, as well as in conformity with her upbringing, Beauvoir gave the 'head' priority. The rational, intellectual bias colours her assessment of women's condition, as well as the path to independence which she charts in *The Second Sex*.

Significantly, in the passage quoted above, it is against herself that Simone directs her resentment, not against Sartre, who is implicated in her tangled feelings. Her body is her femininity, that part of her which needs to be tamed. Only by repressing its desires, by an effort of self-control, can the rational, conscious side of her which plays a role in the world be dominant.

Sartre's relationship to female sexuality remained, throughout his life, an ambivalent one. He loved women, felt that their sensibility made them far preferable as companions to men. He also needed to win them over, feel that they had singled him out beyond other men as objects of their desire. But once seduced, once the woman in question had succumbed to him at a fundamental level, he was no longer sexually interested in her. Indeed, throughout his philosophical and fictional writings, there is a kind of repugnance for the flesh, the mythical terrain of the feminine, a fear of all that is culturally linked to female sexuality. Sartre has a terror of being engulfed, of being swallowed. His work is full of allusions to the nauseous, swamp-like, moist and viscous character of the bodily against which he posits the hard, sharp clarity of the intellect as an antidote. Despite the warmth of his personality, Sartre, as he himself admitted, was cold. He was at once insensitive to and contemptuous of any kind of physical transport which might master a dominant consciousness. This extended beyond sexuality to a relationship with his own body. During his many illnesses, he was all but unaware of his own pain, so great was his will to self-control.

Despite her far more passionate nature, in this respect Simone was effectively Sartre's double. In part because of her own cultural formation, in part because of Sartre's philosophical and personal influence over her, she too despised the prison of the body and its desires and gave primacy to the intellect. Trapped in a Cartesian split between mind and body, between the rational and the irrational, she time and again warned against the physical and sexual bonds which fetter freedom, particularly, as she experienced it, for women.

In her monumental autobiography, Beauvoir gives short shrift to those feelings which would, if allowed free rein, rupture the relationship she and Sartre had embarked on. She is, in effect, constructing an exemplary life of her past in which her heroine is herself. This heroine, as she says time and again, has a gift for happiness: 'I have never met anyone in the whole of my life, who was so well equipped for happiness as I was, or who laboured so stubbornly to achieve it. No sooner had I caught a glimpse of it than I concentrated upon nothing else.' In order to maintain the happiness of her union with Sartre, a union which she termed the great success of her life, Beauvoir stubbornly concentrated on its positive side. Just as there were certain things she could not discuss with him in this most honest and open of relationships, so there are certain evasions in this most honest of autobiographies.

Rarely in the autobiography does she do more than hint at any change in her union with Sartre occasioned by the advent of 'contingent' relationships. Her own jealousy is skimmed over, relegated to the place of an incongruous emotion. In her struggle to live up to their original pact, to behave in as seemingly rational a way as Sartre, the male, Simone de Beauvoir represses, forgets, omits, evades a constellation of concerns which is central to her fictional writing. But the fiction, as we will see later, leaves us in little doubt about the difficulties to which her pact with Sartre led. Throughout her fictional writing, jealousy and particularly jealousy amongst women, is a central theme, as are the vagaries of women in love.

There is something heroic in the young Simone taking on the challenge of a relationship in which she was instantly confronted by rather more of a certain kind of 'independence' than she had bargained for. At the same time, Sartre was himself a little surprised at her acceptance of his schema of necessary and contingent loves. Before meeting Simone and indeed after, he was always at pains to assert his independence from any individual woman and claim his total freedom. As he later ironically admitted, it was hardly necessary then: it was on the whole he who did the chasing. No woman had yet wanted to imprison him in her jealous love. He had already made his speech about the freedom necessary to the great man on several different occasions and met with little success. With Simone, 'I was caught at my own game' he writes in his *Carnets de la drôle de guerre*. The Beaver accepted the freedom he insisted on and became its custodian. Sartre notes that he was fool enough to succumb to a certain melancholy, rather than to recognize his extraordinary good fortune.

'I never knew how properly to lead my sexual nor my sentimental life,' he states with his customary self-critical manner. 'I feel myself sincerely and profoundly to be a bastard . . . a kind of academic sadist, a clerkly Don Juan, to the point of making one retch.' Throughout their lives Simone was to serve as his 'moral conscience', his 'little judge'.

Initially what Sartre proposed to Simone was a two-year contract. During which time they would not take advantage of their agreed-upon freedom, but would give themselves whole-heartedly to their new intimacy – though not under the same roof. (Sartre was to spend eighteen of those months doing his military service as a meteorologist in Tours.) After this they would live apart for two or three years: he had hopes of a post in Japan. By no means was their relationship to be allowed to degenerate into duty or habit. Beauvoir records that, although this instant mention of separation, hot on the heels of Sartre's proposal, caused her some qualms, she trusted Sartre enough to know that he meant what he said when he proclaimed that nothing would prevail against their alliance.

In the event, nothing did. Despite the moments of unhappiness, far more numerous and keenly felt, it would appear, on Simone's part, despite an emotional dependence on Sartre which sometimes flew in the face of her professed beliefs, despite the very real jealousies, the ruptures and 'contingent' loves, Simone de Beauvoir and Jean-Paul Sartre stayed together until the end. I can only admire a tenacity which accepted so much bad with so much good. However, it is clear that on several occasions it fell to Simone to reinfuse with vitality a relationship which the ever-promiscuous Sartre might have abandoned.

Yet there is no doubt that Sartre valued this most 'essential' of relationships. The marvellous thing about the Beaver, Sartre was often to repeat, is that she has the intelligence of a man and the sensibility of a woman. In her he found everything he could possibly desire of a woman. She was the most intimate of friends and this friendship in which all values, all thoughts and all tastes were shared in common,

was renewed by constant invention. The result of this 'federation' was an overwhelming happiness.

Throughout this 'federation', Simone was his foremost
critic and editor. Sartre's entire philosophical œuvre is dedicated to her. Once Simone had given her imprimatur to any
of his ideas or writings, no other critic counted. 'One could
say that I write for her or more exactly so that she can filter
the work.' The philosophical treatise which was to become
La Nausée, Sartre's most popular book, took on its fictional
form because of Simone's intervention. No sooner did the
couple meet – even after long absences – than their philosophical dialogue recommenced. 'There is a deep relation
between us,' Sartre commented in 1977, 'which at moments creates what is almost a single individuality, a "we"
which is not two "yous", but really a "we". I have had this
"we" throughout my life with Simone de Beauvoir.'

The longevity of the Sartre-Beauvoir relationship is even
more remarkable in that the couple, in accordance with
their original pact, remained unmarried and childless. On
the one occasion when Sartre suggested they might marry
so that Simone, anxious about an imminent separation,
might be offered a post in the same city as he (married
couples could be offered double teaching posts by the state),
Simone instantly refused. To bow to institutions and social
pressure would be against her and Sartre's then anarchist
principles. Also, as Beauvoir writes, 'Marriage doubles one's
domestic responsibilities, and, indeed, all one's social
chores.'

In the rest of her explanation of why she refused to marry
Sartre, however, there is a suggestion that she did so not so

much for herself, but because she feared the effect it might have on a Sartre who 'had thrown himself so wholeheartedly into the business of being young that when his youth would finally leave him he would need strong attachments indeed to afford him consolation'.

I could see how much it cost Sartre to bid farewell to his travels, his own freedom, his youth – in order to become a provincial academic, now fully and forever grown-up. To have joined the ranks of the married men would have meant an even greater renunciation. I knew he was incapable of bearing a grudge against me; but I knew, too, how vulnerable I was to the prick of conscience, and how greatly I detested it.

This Sartre who refuses manhood may also in part explain Simone's decision never to have children – something she had envisaged as an integral part of an imagined union with her cousin, Jacques. The Sartre who is everything to Simone is also in some respects her child, the being she will look after until his death, whose health she worries over and whose welfare she tends to even when he behaves irresponsibly.

Beauvoir herself had thought this question through, as is true of so many of the questions we are tempted to ask of her. But as in so many of those matters which deal specifically with her place as a woman, her autobiography skirts over the difficulties. The refusal of maternity may well have engendered rather more turmoil at some point in her life than she is prepared to acknowledge. In her vehement desire for happiness, her need to accommodate Sartre's wishes – and in retrospect to mythologize their union – Simone largely allows only answerable doubts to surface. She sees childbearing as a purposeless and unjustifiable increase of the world's population, motherhood as a contradiction to her literary vocation which 'would not admit impediments'. Unlike her friend Zaza, she does not see having a child as a vital creative task equal to writing. And finally,

A child would not have strengthened the bonds that united Sartre and me; nor did I want Sartre's existence reflected and extended in some other being. He was sufficient both for himself and for me. I too was self-sufficient: I never once dreamed of rediscovering myself in the child I might bear. In any case, I felt such absence of affinity with my own parents that any sons or daughters I might have I regarded in advance as strangers . . . So I had no dream urging me to embrace maternity: and to look at it another way, maternity itself seemed incompatible with the way of life upon which I was embarking. I knew that in order to become a writer I needed a great measure of time and freedom.

Beauvoir's reasoning is impeccable and I am almost persuaded. Certainly, given the trajectory of her rebellion against bourgeois conventions and her move into independence, the rejection of maternity is logical. At the same time, it seems equally clear that if Sartre had wanted children, Beauvoir would have reconsidered. But as it was, Sartre remained sufficient.

For Simone, this man whom she continued to address with the formal *vous* throughout her life, this man, from whose familial home she was ostracized until the death of Sartre's step-father, remained her double. They wore an identical sign on their brows. 'The comradeship that welded our lives together made a superfluous mockery of any other bond we might have forged for ourselves.'

THREE

Literature As Salvation

From 1929 when she left her parents' home to establish an independent existence until 1941 when *She Came to Stay* was finished, Simone de Beauvoir's life was an extended literary apprenticeship. For Beauvoir and Sartre, to write was a primary injunction, the single activity which gave purpose and meaning to life. The only goal of an absurd existence was to produce works of art. This dedication to literature – which bears the traces of Beauvoir and Sartre's formation in the early twentieth-century ethos of the modernist movement – did not always prove easy for Simone. In the early days of her relationship with Sartre, she was too immersed in the all-consuming business of being happy to be able to work with any conviction. Released from the constraints of her family, the rules and regulations which governed respectable bourgeois life, Simone threw herself with reckless abandon into the activity of living. When questioned about his daughter, her father would say, Simone is having her Paris honeymoon.

The cinema, the cafés frequented by the artistic avant-garde, dance clubs, even brothels – that low life so loved by

Bohemian Paris – became Simone de Beauvoir's regular haunts. This artists' Paris was also an international Paris. The Chilean poet Huidburo sat side by side with the painter Robert Delaunay, the composer Varèse and visiting writers from Madrid and Budapest. They railed against human stupidity or dreamt up outlandish plots – such as illuminating the Eiffel Tower with a sign that read MERDE. With a shop girl she had taken a liking to, Simone powdered her face a deathly white, painted her lips blood red and went dancing. Her favourite partner was a young butcher's assistant.

White nights were succeeded by exhausted days in which the work of teaching had somehow to be got through. Particularly on Mondays, after a weekend spent with Sartre in Tours, where he was doing his military service, and long journeys on overcrowded trains, Simone would drop from fatigue.

The intoxication of love, of new-found friends, the sheer joy of living, all this made writing something of a drudgery. Too much of a puritan to give up the idea of serious work altogether, however, Simone agonized about her inability to settle down to her true vocation. It was more than simply a question of time wasted in pleasure. Amidst her newly discovered independence, an inner and sexual dependence on Sartre had left Simone with nothing of herself and with nothing to say. 'I had ceased to exist on my own account, and was now a mere parasite.'

This problematic situation, typical of the one she describes as the condition of the woman in love in *The Second Sex*, was exacerbated by the fact that the last thing Sartre wanted was a *dependent* woman. He felt anxious about Simone, re-proached her for no longer having ideas. He told her to watch out against becoming a female introvert.

There was, indeed, no danger of my turning into a mere housewife, but he compared me to those heroines of Meredith's who after a long battle for their independence ended up quite content to be some man's helpmeet. I was furious with myself for disappointing him in this way ... I reflected that to adapt one's outlook to another person's salvation is the surest and quickest way of losing him.

Simone de Beauvoir is quick to point out that she did not at that time understand her problem as arising from the fact that she was a woman. 'To accept a secondary status in life, that of a merely ancillary being, would have been to degrade my own humanity; and my entire past rose up in protest against such a step.' Nonetheless, the experience fed her understanding of the subject matter which was to form her most influential book, *The Second Sex*.

Simone was not able to establish that inner self-confidence she needed to write until she had determined on a period of separation from Sartre. After his term of military service came to an end, Sartre's hopes for a post in Japan fell through. In the French education system appointments for teaching posts are made by a central administration. Sartre in 1931 was appointed to a post in Le Havre. Simone was relieved. The separation she had dreaded and yet agreed to with Sartre was not to be. But close on the heels of Sartre's appointment to his post conveniently close to Paris, came notice of a place for Simone in Marseilles. She was thrown into a state of panic. It was one thing to dream of a solitude in which she would dedicate herself to work, another to have it arrive as a tangible reality. Sartre offered marriage as an escape. Simone refused, forcing herself to hold fast to her original pact with Sartre and to her youthful ideas about the virtues of being alone. She could not let herself succumb to the very real danger of sacrificing her independence for love.

Looking back, she was to feel that her arrival in Marseilles marked a turning point in her life. Forced to rely on her own devices, Simone began to lead a life which shocked her fellow professionals. Her classes strayed from the prescribed curriculum to include Simone's thoughts on work and justice, the nature of capital and colonialism. She talked about Gide and Proust, provoking parents' complaints about immorality and earning her reprimands from superiors. In provincial Marseilles, her conduct itself was seen as scandalous. It was still something of a novelty in those days for a woman to do things alone: Simone did everything alone. Shunning the company of her colleagues, she sat in restaurants and cafés on her own, and wrote endlessly. She went to the cinema alone and walked through the streets of unsavoury neighbourhoods near the large port. Even more unseemly was the fact that she went for long hikes on her own, against shrill warnings of inevitable rape. These solitary rambles in the countryside outside Marseilles became an obsession. She would plan intricate routes and fearlessly thumb lifts at a time when hitch-hiking was unheard of, and then scramble for whole days through the hills and valleys of the Lubéron, sometimes covering as much as forty kilometres. This passion for walking stayed with her until age and health made it impossible. Despite Sartre's criticism, Simone never lost her near-mystical sense of oneness with nature, to which Sartre's approach was akin to that of an intellectual vivisectionist. Country rambles were never his passion.

As well as provoking outrage, Simone's behaviour also earned her the admiration of a few select students and a homosexual approach from one of her fellow teachers, which took her completely by surprise. Yet everything that happened to her in this year in Marseilles fascinated her. She was indulging herself in a process of narcissistic self-observation. With time on her hands, she began a new novel. As in all her early books, both failed and completed, her theme was 'the mirage of the other'. More than a philosophical problem, this threat that others posed was a personal experience. Her habit of cautious isolation sprang from her fear of others, a 'refusal to envisage other people as potential individuals with consciences like myself'. It was a refusal which could not but affect her fiction where the imaginative act of being other precedes any intellectual capactiy for embodying philosophical problems in character.

During these years of literary apprenticeship, Simone was far more successful as a critic for Sartre than as a writer. His pamphlet on contingency, which Simone read on one of her trips to Paris from Marseilles, contained the germ of *Nausea*. Simone suggested that he transform this lengthy abstract dissertation into a fiction and infuse his narrative with the suspense they both so enjoyed in thrillers. She criticized his work with meticulous severity. Sartre, as always, took her advice.

Both Sartre and Simone at this time were opposed to any intrusion of politics into literature, something of an irony given their later development. Any form of political or social engagement seemed as vain as religion. When Simone attempted to get a Paris job with the militant feminist Louise Weiss who ran the review, *L'Europe Nouvelle*, the latter found her ideas on politics and the rights of women far too vague, whereas Simone was intimidated by the older woman's militant approach.

During the thirties, Sartre and Simone saw themselves as individualist anarchists, if a name had to be put to it. They knew what they were against – existing social institutions, bourgeois hypocrisy, the lie of religion – but they had no distinct programme of their own. Nor would they identify themselves with any of the left groups to whom they were in various respects sympathetic. They saw literature as the terrain of imaginative freedom, certainly not of any sectarian politics. They were critical of their friend, Paul Nizan, who was a member of the Communist Party and whose novels put the class struggle in the forefront.

We did not regard ourselves as wholly uninvolved. We aimed to make an active personal contribution through our discussions, our teaching and our books: such a contribution would be critical rather than constructive, but at this particular moment, we felt that criticism had a most important role to fulfil.

It was to take another ten years and the experience of World War II for personal radicalism and a belief in literature to be transformed into social engagement and the idea of a literature of commitment.

*

In 1932 Simone de Beauvoir was appointed to a teaching post in Rouen, far closer to the Paris she missed and to Sartre. Colette Audry, a friend and fellow teacher remembers the twenty-four-year-old Simone:

She seemed to us excessively well brought up, except for her raucous and rapid speech . . . Gifted with solid appetites and an exceptional ardour in work and play, she transformed every minute into an instance of happiness . . . She had started one book, was dissatisfied with it, left her draft to start on another and then bravely, yet another. Her courage had no limits. She would be a writer. There was no doubt about that neither for her, nor for us.

In Rouen Simone made her headquarters a small unpopular brasserie, where the lack of customers permitted her to write at her leisure. Another novel, this time a chronicle which prefigures *The Mandarins*, was begun and then abandoned. Meanwhile she and Sartre continued their unending dialogue – whether in Paris, Rouen or Le Havre. With an aplomb which later seemed far too great, they blithely rejected all existing theories, whether psychoanalytical or political, but as yet had nothing to put in their place. Their favourite activity, which was intended as food for fiction, consisted of analysing others. As she herself admits, Beauvoir often judged without understanding. She was still both indifferent to and threatened by others.

As in Marseilles, both her teaching and her life style provoked criticism. The Regional Commission for the Protection of Children had sent out a directive to teachers proclaiming that girls should be taught to think of maternity as their proper destiny. Simone rebelled. She was put on the school's black list. In her passionate written defence, she attacked not only the Regional Commission, but the students' parents as well for their Nazi sympathies.

In the autumn of 1933 Sartre went to Berlin to acquaint himself at first hand with phenomenology. He sent letters to Simone describing Hitler's rise to power, the mass demonstrations and riots, anti-semitism and press censorship. Simone, still ferociously dedicated to happiness and, like many of her generation, unwilling to conceive of the possibility of another war, turned a blind eye to politics. In her autobiography, she chastises herself for her own escapism, but as she explains, at that time she wanted people to despise the futile contingencies of daily life. This stubborn dedication to indifference benefited neither her fiction, which went badly, nor her state of mind. During Sartre's absence, she grew depressed with her lack of achievement: 'No husband, no children, no home, social polish and twenty-six years old: when you reach this age you want to feel your feet on the ground.'

On top of this growing dissatisfaction with her own state, Simone learned from Sartre that he had fallen in love with the wife of a colleague of his. This, the first of his 'amours passionnels' – passionate loves, rather than mere sexual exploits – since their union was established brought Simone quickly to Berlin. Her autobiographical note on the matter hints again at an attempt to rationalize her emotions. It is just a little too matter-of-fact:

... this affair took me neither by surprise nor upset any notions I had formed concerning our joint lives, since right from the outset Sartre had warned me that he was liable to embark on such adventures. I had accepted the principle, and now I had no difficulty in accepting the fact . . . Besides, I felt so closely bound to him that no such episode in his life could disturb me.

With all her dedication to their joint project 'to know the world and give it expression', Simone could not but be disturbed by the next of Sartre's infatuations. But the disturbance proved to be precisely what she needed to set her literary ambitions truly into motion.

When Sartre initially returned from Berlin to Le Havre, his and Simone's lives began once again to move in well-trodden paths. Simone fell into a depression. She was nearing thirty and the excitement of all the discoveries she had made after leaving university was ebbing away. She felt old. If she drank too much, she was liable to burst into floods of tears. Sartre railed against her, telling her it was wrong to explain her condition in terms of metaphysics when in fact it was alcohol which caused her depressions. Meanwhile Sartre, probably as a result of the mescalin with which he was experimenting, began to suffer regularly from hallucinations. His visual faculties became distorted and he began to imagine that houses gnashed their jaws at him as he walked past, that he was being followed by lobsters. He thought he was going mad.

Underlying his state was a dissatisfaction as great if not greater than Simone's. She at least, she writes, had him – 'his mere existence justified the world'. For him, however, their union, even without the sanction of marriage, signified a curtailment of freedom. Their future seemed to be progressing along a pre-ordained path. Moreover, teaching for Sartre had always been intended as a half-way house and he felt himself trapped in an institutional world which for Simone, as a woman, signified one hurdle crossed on the road to independence. Then, too, Sartre's writing, despite his frenetic dedication to it, was slow in being accepted by publishers and in gaining him recognition. His depression persisted.

Simone, with her sound common sense, her blindness to psychology, and her all but hysterical determination to be happy, to see the bright side of things, tried to snap him out of it. She couldn't believe in the reality of his fears and delusions. After all, for her Sartre represented 'pure mind and radical freedom'. She regarded his new bleak passivity as a kind of treachery. But neither her assiduous reasoning nor the travel they enjoyed together in other circumstances acted as more than a temporary remedy.

It was during this black period that Olga Kosakiewicz began to serve as Sartre's nurse and companion when he visited Rouen. Olga Kosakiewicz was a student of Beauvoir's at the *Lycée* in Rouen. Pretty, impetuous, rebellious, she became for Sartre and Simone the very embodiment of the youth that was slipping through their fingers. Olga lived only for the moment; all striving and perserverance – the very characteristics which singled out Simone de Beauvoir and had brought her to her present place – she considered contemptible. Only the moment, emotions, and extreme sensations counted for her.

In Olga's presence Sartre's persecuting crustaceans vanished. As Beauvoir writes, 'the vast empty beach they left behind them [was] all ready to be filled with new obsessional fancies'. Simone preferred Sartre's obsession with Olga's every glance and gesture to his slow collapse from some hallucinatory psychosis. Or so she thought at first.

When Olga failed the exams which would have taken her off to the medical school of her parents' choice, Sartre and Beauvoir decided to 'adopt' her. With her parents' permission, Simone became Olga's director of studies, Sartre her philosophy professor. But tutoring Olga, the most agreeable of companions, was not an easy task. Her indolence triumphed over any attempt at systematic study. Rather than a student, she took on the aura of Sartre's and Simone's 'enfant terrible', a mythical creature they invested with properties at once angelic and demonic.

It has been said that for Sartre and Beauvoir, Olga was the child they never had: that third person who comes along at once to infuse new life into a relationship and to disrupt its accumulated habits: '. . . it struck us as being both opportune and flattering to our self-esteem to put ourselves out on behalf of a young person who might profit from our care. Her clumsy inability to cope with life gave Olga a claim on our assistance; and in return she gave our already stale world some much needed freshening up.' Beauvoir's use of the plural 'we' in her reflections, I sense, bears witness far more accurately to Sartre's 'I' than to a feeling equally shared. The adoption of Olga carried a sting in its tail directed at Simone rather than Sartre. His infatuation with the young Russian became so great that Simone felt displaced. In the Sartre who admired Olga and was captive to her opinions, Simone could no longer find the man whose ideas and values she had been at one with. Sartre was inhabited by a terrifying 'other'.

The situation was exacerbated by the fact that Simone was intellectually committed to the idea of a trio. Sartre and she had long toyed with the notion of introducing another consciousness into their twosome so that they were each forced to rediscover themselves and each other through the gaze of an outsider. The reality, however, had rather different ramifications than the projections she had imagined.

On a day-to-day level, it was Olga who called the tune, she who decided whether she would see Simone, whom she admired greatly and in some ways preferred to Sartre, or Sartre – which had the advantage of making Simone jealous and her more desirable in Simone's eyes. Or they could do things as a trio.

Simone began to feel trapped. She wanted to hear neither of the other two's narratives or plaints about their experience with the other. Nor, dedicated as she was to Sartre, could she envisage the trio extending itself into the future, something which Sartre wanted. The hothouse atmosphere, the inevitable voyeurism, the very real intellectual advantage Sartre and Beauvoir had over the young Olga – in many ways the victim of their endless dissecting analyses – Sartre's extreme moods which fluctuated between frenzied alarm and an ecstasy Simone had never awakened in him – all this produced in Simone a misery which went far beyond mere jealousy: '... at times I asked myself whether the whole of my happiness did not rest upon a gigantic lie.'

Inveterately rational, self-admittedly a bad psychologist, isolated from anyone outside the trio, Simone could neither understand what was happening nor control it. She succumbed to a despair greater than any she had previously felt. 'When [Olga] stood apart from me she looked at me with alien eyes, and I was transformed into an *object* that might be either idol or enemy.' That hell which is other people was beginning to close in. And Sartre, too, was no longer part of a 'we', but had become other, so distinct from himself that he began to doubt the possibility of salvation through literature, the very premise of his union with Simone.

I can only imagine that Olga's unspoken misery must have been equal to Simone's. One evening when the trio went out together she pressed a lighted cigarette into her hand 'with positively maniacal concentration'. Simone calls this act an aberration, but beneath the wilful gesture, the pain of being imprisoned in the trio, the call for help is evident.

It was Olga who made the first move to break up the trio by entering into a relationship with the attractive Jacques-Laurent Bost, a student and friend of Sartre's – the kind of youth, Sartre said, for whom he wanted to 'reinvent man'. The trio's move to Paris where Simone was now teaching at the lycée Molière, while Sartre commuted from near-by Laon, had not altered what had become an infernal triangle. Olga's gesture, however, was only half-hearted and it took Simone's escape into illness to mark the next step towards the trio's eventual dissolution.

Always prone to masking her misery by driving herself to more work and greater expenditure of energy, during the autumn and winter term of 1936–7 Simone had pushed herself beyond even her formidable endurance. She had been working for a long time now on the linked stories which comprise *When Things of the Spirit Come First* – her final attempt to expose 'the multitude of crimes ... which hide behind a veil of spiritual hocus-pocus' – and was anxious to finish the book. Either with Olga or Sartre or both, she tended to stay up very late at night and would then rise early and rush off to the *lycée*.

Exhaustion took its toll. Simone collapsed with pneumonia, was instantly hospitalized and hovered for many days between consciousness and unconsciousness before an extended convalescence began. She vowed that she would now change her life. As soon as she was well enough, she fled to her beloved Provence and little by little slipped back into her routine of day long rambles. Nature had always had a healing influence on her, enabling her at once to lose herself in her surroundings and to remake herself afresh. But in Paris little had changed and it took two more decisive steps to put the affair with Olga finally to rest. Both were important landmarks on Simone's path to inner independence.

For the eight years since she and Sartre had sealed their pact, Simone had watched him take advantage of 'contingent loves' while she remained locked in a dependent faithfulness and a recurrent jealous anxiety. Now, after her illness and in the midst of the ordeal of the trio with Olga, Simone finally asserted her own sexuality and engaged on a relationship with Bost. There is no question but that this affair bore the traces of a revenge, an attempt on Simone's part to re-establish an equilibrium which Sartre's infatuation with Olga had savagely disrupted. Equally, this somewhat incestuous squaring of a triangle allowed Simone to achieve a new confidence, a measure of greater independence. Evidence has it that Sartre was pleased at the step, but even his calm, paternalistic sanction couldn't erase the fact that Simone had acted on her own, had nervously propositioned the young Bost during one of those arduous mountain treks on which only he could follow the intrepid Beaver.

The second milestone on Simone's journey, perhaps the more significant one, lies in her broaching a novel which bore an intimate relation to her own *emotional*, as well as intellectual, concerns: *She Came to Stay*, the book which gives fictional life to the experience of the trio and depicts the turmoil engendered in a stable relationship by the arrival of a third party.

1937 found both Simone and Sartre at last in Paris. A Montparnasse hotel in which he lived on the floor above her, served as home: 'thus we had all the advantages of a shared life without any of its inconveniences.' Simone, in the way she then had of searching for subjects, was worrying about what to write next. It was Sartre who propelled her in the necessary direction:

'Look,' he said, with sudden vehemence, 'why don't you put *yourself* into your writing? . . . I felt as though someone had banged me hard on the head. 'I'd never dare to do that,' I said. To put my raw, undigested self into a book, to lose perspective, compromise myself – no, I couldn't do it, I found the whole idea terrifying. 'Screw up your courage,' Sartre told me, and kept pressing the point. I had my own individual emotions and reactions; it was these that I ought to express in my writings. As happened whenever he put himself behind a plan, his words conjured up a host of possibilities and hopes; but I was still afraid. What in fact was I afraid of? It seemed to me that from the moment I began to nourish literature with the stuff of my own personality, it would become something as serious as happiness or death.

At the moment that she took up the challenge of self-exposure, and placed her writing on a plane as dangerous as life itself, Simone crossed over the threshold from literary apprenticeship to being a writer and simultaneously put paid to the trio. *She Came to Stay* took almost three years to complete and went through many drafts. 'In this novel I exposed myself so dangerously that at times the gap between my emotions and the words to express them seemed insurmountable ... If I was to overcome *on my own account* that solitary wilderness into which I had flung Françoise [her heroine], I must work my fantasy through to the bitter end.' This is precisely what Simone did in *She Came to Stay*, perhaps in more ways than she was aware.

Françoise, a writer, and Pierre, a theatre director with whom she works, have an open and satisfying relationship which is threatened by Pierre's growing interest in Xavière, a seductive and impetuous younger woman whom the couple have informally adopted. Initially a friend and protegée of Françoise's, who is happy to welcome her into a duo which takes freedom as its basic principle, Xavière's selfishness and growing flirtation with Pierre gradually thrusts Françoise into agonies of jealousy. She finds this emotional morass shameful and inappropriate to the chosen nature of their relationship. It makes her akin to the minor character, Elizabeth, who is tortured by jealousy, in part because her concealed inner life is empty. For Françoise to admit to jealousy, for Françoise to prevent Pierre, who is increasingly obsessed by Xavière, from seeing her, would be to give way to the arid conventions of bourgeois marriage. Yet what the intellect prescribes is often not in keeping with experienced emotions. Caught in an impossible contradiction between what she feels and how she thinks she should behave, Françoise retreats into a delirious illness, at once masochistically leaving the ground free for Pierre and Xavière to consummate their love and signalling her need for sympathy. This strategy fails. Françoise then engages on an affair with the young actor, Gerbert. But this escape from the claustrophobia of the incestuous threesome is viewed as an act of revenge by Xavière. Françoise feels suffocated by being compelled to confront an image of herself that she cannot accept. In order to destroy the image she sees in Xavière's eyes, in Pierre's absence she turns on the gas and abandons the sleeping Xavière to die.

Significantly Pierre, the Sartre character, is all but a shadow in the novel. Beauvoir, always a ready critic of herself, admits that this is one of the book's failings, but, she explains, she was 'loathe to offer the public a portrait of Sartre as I knew him'. Protecting Sartre from exposure, she also shields the Pierre character from any criticism. Françoise never confronts Pierre with what in the novel emerges quite clearly as childish and selfish behaviour. Nor does Françoise, so cool in her self-analysis otherwise, admit to the rage and resentment which runs through the entirety of the book. Instead of pointing a finger at him, she turns on Xavière.

In Simone de Beauvoir's own statement about the book, she claims that its germ lay in a philosophical problem which had obsessed her for many years. How is one to come to terms with the rational awareness possessed by other people, the irreducible actuality of a personality alien to oneself? If the other has a full consciousness equal to one's own, then her view could annihilate one's self perception, one's very existence. As Sartre was to put it so succinctly in a later work, hell is other people. Françoise refuses to be that woman she imagines Xavière sees her as. The shame is too great. 'It is she or I,' she says to herself. So she annihilates the other. Françoise had made a choice and acted upon it. In that action lies freedom.

To make a choice between freedom and constraint is one of the basic tenets upon which Sartre and Beauvoir's early philosophy of existentialism rests. Constraint is what convention imposes upon one, freedom is what one creates through action. In terms of a chosen love relationship, this becomes translated into an injunction never to circumscribe the freedom of the other person in a couple, never to make limiting claims. With this axiomatic starting point, Françoise in *She Came to Stay* cannot make any demands of Pierre; she can only annihilate that other who threatens to destroy her own and the couple's freedom: Xavière.

Whilst in one sense the novel gives concrete human form to a philosophical hypothesis, it is also a testimony to the kind of difficulties, the agony of jealousy, Simone experienced in her relationship with Sartre. Significantly in neither the novel nor her autobiography is she prepared to call into question the relationship between Pierre and Françoise, Sartre and herself. Instead, anger, revenge are turned towards the other woman.

The pattern of jealousy which sees rage against the male turned instead against the other woman is a prevalent one in Beauvoir's work. In *The Mandarins*, the hero, Henri, frees himself blamelessly and with relative ease from his jealous mistress of many years. As readers, our sympathy is evoked on his behalf rather than on that of his mistress, Paule. *All Men are Mortal* begins with the heroine's malicious act against a fellow actress of whom she is jealous. In her last fiction, *The Woman Destroyed*, Beauvoir explicitly invokes the ageing jealous wife as a figure to be criticized. As *The Second Sex* emphasizes, for Beauvoir jealousy is the inevitable condition of the dependent woman trapped by love:

Woman . . . loving her man in his alterity and in his transcendence, feels in danger at every moment. There is no great distance between the treason of absence and infidelity. From the moment when she feels less than perfectly loved, she becomes jealous, and in view of her demands, this is always pretty much the case; her reproaches and complaints, whatever the pretexts, come to the surface in jealous scenes; she will express in the very impatience and ennui of waiting, the bitter taste of her dependence, her regret at having only a mutilated existence. Her entire destiny is involved in each glance her lover casts at another woman, since she has identified her whole being with him.

Given this understanding of the archetypal woman in love, it is hardly surprising that Simone de Beauvoir prefers to skirt over and rationalize any jealousy she herself may have felt and certainly keep it hidden from Sartre. In their love, a relationship based on the mutual recognition of two liberties, there was no place for such archaic emotions. Yet the theme of love remains her foremost fictional concern. Whether she is ostensibly embarking on a novelistic exploration of the morality of resistance during the French Occupation, as in *The Blood of Others*, the necessity of commitment in *All Men are Mortal*, or French political and intellectual life in the post World War II era in *The Mandarins*, it is the evocation of women in love, unhappily in love, which gives the books their lasting vitality.

Despite the varying success of her later work in its elaborations of the theme of love and jealousy, *She Came to Stay*, because of the very rawness of its emotion, remains in many ways Beauvoir's most compelling novel. Whatever its lack of novelistic artfulness, the murder of Xavière/Olga and the path leading to it have a kind of bitter inexorability – almost as if Beauvoir weren't, for once, in charge of her material.

This is almost certainly due to the fact that it is not only the conscious fantasy of Xavière/Olga's murder that Beauvoir realizes in *She Came to Stay*. The book also works through a whole cluster of unconscious fantasies and these give the novel its particularly claustrophobic and incestuous density. If Simone is Françoise, at once mother and rival to Xavière/Olga in her relationship to the Pierre/Sartre character, she is also Xavière, that daughter who was jealous of her mother in their rivalry for the father's *essential* love. Françoise was, of course, Simone's own mother's name and the presence of the parental duo in the book may account for the lack of any overt sexual relationship between them. Understanding the book in part as an Oedipal, family romance also helps to explain the particular pattern of jealousy between women which Beauvoir time and again explores. It is mother and daughter who battle over the distant father, desirable beyond criticism. If in this instance, Beauvoir allows the mother to win, I imagine it is in part an attempt to resolve her own Oedipal desires, her own guilt *vis-à-vis* her mother, and to put the daughter in her to rest. In so doing, she simultaneously frees herself from that childhood self who needs to find in the father an absolute authority on whom her being depends. In writing *She Came to Stay*, her first published novel, Simone marks her growing independence from the paternal Sartre. Literature can act as salvation in a variety of guises.

Before it could do so for Simone, something in her life had had to go seriously wrong. Her complacent sense of reality had had to be shattered. 'Literature is born when something in life goes slightly adrift,' she writes in her autobiography. During her years of apprenticeship, she was so 'blinded with sheer happiness' that there was no urge to escape from her blissful condition. 'My schemes of work remained futile dreams till the day came when that happiness was threatened and I rediscovered a certain kind of solitude in anxiety. The unfortunate episode of the trio did much more than supply me with a subject for a novel; it enabled me to deal with it.' Throughout her life Beauvoir's writing grew out of life crises. *The Blood of Others*, *The Second Sex*, *The Mandarins*, *A Very Easy Death*, *Old Age*, and *Adieux – A Farewell to Sartre* can best be read at once as symptoms of such crises and their resolution.

By 1941 when *She Came to Stay* was finished, Simone's universe had been fractured once again: this time by much more than the matter of a 'contingent love'.

FOUR

The Ethics of Existentialism

In the years leading into the Second World War Simone de Beauvoir at last began to recognize that her refusal of politics itself constituted a political attitude. She shared this attitude with a great number of the very people she otherwise sought to disassociate herself from. Like them, in her pursuit of personal happiness, she blinded herself to the signs of encroaching war. The change in her began when a friend, visiting from Spain, gave her a full account of the horrors of the Civil War there and the effects of Franco's seizure of power. He pointed an implicating finger at the French: if the French government had acted in 1936, rather than adopting a politics of non-intervention, the Republic might have been saved. Beauvoir felt personally attacked.

As news began to filter through from Germany proclaiming the existence of concentration camps where millions of anti-fascists and Jews were interned, Beauvoir began to realize that political passivity was no longer a possible position. Up until this time her energetic quest for happiness had characterized Simone's life. Her greed for seeing, reading and understanding, for eating and travelling through France, through Spain, Italy, London, whenever and wherever possible, her almost ferocious lust for experience was proverbial amongst her friends. Beneath the incessant activity, lay a very real fear of death, the horror of that boundless emptiness which had made her scream out loud when in adolescence she had lost her belief in God. The terror of death, of an abandoned universe unredeemed by consciousness and hence meaning, haunted her throughout her life. War – and she was pursued in the late 1930s by visions of the First World War – would bring death in its train, the death of many of her friends, particularly the younger ones like Bost. This at first seemed to her far worse a fate than the possible political change that an invading government might bring. She argued with Sartre: 'Surely a France at war would be worse than France under the Nazis.' Sartre, always more tempted by active politics than she had been, replied, 'I have no desire to eat my manuscripts.' He was convinced that war could no longer be avoided. Sometime in the spring of 1939, Simone finally agreed with him. This was the year which marked an end to what she calls her individualist, anti-humanist way of life. Simone began to learn the value of solidarity.

In retrospect, the preceding years of her life seemed to have been marked by a total lack of reality, not simply because of the sheltered security of her and Sartre's existence, whatever its surface unconventionality, but because of her own 'bourgeois idealism, aestheticism and universalist abstractions' which blinded her to the politics of her time and to the inevitability of war.

Then, suddenly, History burst over me, and I dissolved into fragments. I woke to find myself scattered over the four quarters of the globe, linked by every nerve in me to each and every other individual. All my ideas and values were turned upside down; even the pursuit of happiness lost its importance.

The Simone de Beauvoir born from these fragments is the woman most usually associated with her name: an active, public intellectual whose morality thrusts aside any ivory-tower aestheticism and sincerely embraces responsibility and just causes. Amongst English writers, it is perhaps only George Eliot who bears a kinship to Simone de Beauvoir in the insistence of her moral concern.

From September 1939 when war was declared and Sartre drafted until his return in March 1941, having spent the last ten months as a German prisoner of war, Simone de Beauvoir faced the disorientations and panic of the phoney war and the German Occupation alone. Initially, to maintain her sanity, she kept a journal, read ferociously, and with an obsessive intensity gave herself a course in music. Once people had learned how to keep lights on behind panes darkened against potential bombs, she sat every evening at the Dôme or another café writing her journal or endless letters to Sartre and revising *She Came to Stay*. She also carried on teaching. With her characteristic determination and against all the odds, since they weren't married, she managed to obtain a permit which would allow her to visit Sartre. In the twenty-four hours they were granted together, she read the first hundred pages of his *Age of Reason*, while he looked through her diary and again told her to expand her analysis of herself. Simone had begun to ask the questions which form the germ of *The Second Sex*: what sort of woman is she? in what ways is she typically feminine and in what ways not? The war, there is no doubt, gave Simone a sense of commonality: with other women she collected her ration coupons and tried to put meals together. Like them she queued for passes in government offices, waved tearful goodbyes to her man at train stations, and agonized about his return.

In May 1940 the phoney war drew to an end. In rapid succession Holland and Belgium gave way to German troops who then advanced into France. Hitler declared that by 15 June his tanks would be in Paris. On 4 June the Paris area was bombed. Simone's one thought was not to be caught like a rat in an occupied city, cut off from Sartre. Yet she had to remain there to supervise examinations on the 10th. On the 9th, a Jewish friend told her that they had to leave Paris the following day or it could prove too late: the examinations had been cancelled.

With a single suitcase containing all of Sartre's letters to her since 1929, Simone left Paris. The roads were congested: six million people were moving south, fleeing from the Germans. They travelled in cars and lorries, buses and bicycles, horses and carts, or they walked – any means were preferable to staying in Paris. In *The Blood of Others*, her novel about the Resistance, Beauvoir described the nervous frenzy of those days. At Laval, she left her case at a depot and went off to make a telephone call to her place of destination, at one of the few functioning telephones en route. When she returned her suitcase was gone.

On 21 June, the clauses of the armistice were published

and Marshall Pétain's collaborationist government was in place. Simone's depression was tempered by the thought that perhaps now Sartre – if he was alive – would somehow make his way back to Paris. Her only thought was that she too must return to the occupied city, whatever the difficulties. She hitched a lift part of the way and then, when the short supply of civilian petrol ran out, she determined to walk the 110 remaining miles to Paris – despite the fact that there was no food available and a general order that refugees were not to be allowed back into the city where provisions were desperately short. Finally she made her way, in part in the back of a German lorry and finally in a Red Cross car.

Paris in the early days of the German occupation was like a ghost town: closed shops, empty streets, their monotony only broken by the grey and black of German troops or the low-flying aircraft overhead. Simone was in despair: she had learnt that it was most likely that prisoners would not be released until the end of the war. She moved back into her mother's flat which was now empty and went daily to the Bibliothèque Nationale. Here, from two until five every day she read Hegel's *Phenomenology of Mind*. Deciphering its difficulties was the most soothing occupation she could imagine.

At last in mid-July there was a note from Sartre. He was alive. Simone knew that she was one of the lucky ones, though life in occupied Paris weighed heavily on her. At the *Lycée* where she now taught, she had no alternative but to sign a repugnant document swearing that she was neither a Freemason nor a Jew. The Vichy Government, despite its nominal independence, did everything that the Germans ordered. Simone was appalled at the crawling hypocrisy of Pétain: 'They were all lying: these generals and other notables who had sabotaged the war because they preferred Hitler to the Popular Front' – the short-lived alliance of the left which had been in power before the war.

The Marshal's 'messages' attacked everything which I felt to be of value, liberty in particular. Henceforth the family would be the sovereign unit, the reign of virtue was at hand, and God would be spoken of respectfully in the schools. This was something I knew only too well, the same violent prejudice and stupidity that had darkened my childhood – only now it extended over the entire country, an official and repressive blanket.

Fear, rage and a sense of impotence were Simone's responses to the war. In 1941, she was dismissed from her teaching post. The parent of a student protegée (the model for the daughter, Nadine, in *The Mandarins*) had complained to the school authorities that Beauvoir had led her daughter astray. Is there a suggestion here of a lesbian affair? Certainly Beauvoir's writings lead us to believe that she knew something of the nature of homosexual passion. There is, however, no certain proof. All we know is that the student in question, who showed all the signs of being 'in love' with Simone, refused to marry the man of her family's choice. The right-wing administration was not one to sanction unconventional behaviour and teaching remained closed to Simone until after the war.

What the experience of war provoked in both Beauvoir and Sartre was a sense of responsibility and solidarity – the two foundation stones of existentialist morality. No longer did they see their condition as a unique one: 'In occupied France,' Beauvoir writes, 'the mere fact of being alive implied acquiescence in oppression. Not even suicide would have freed me from this dilemma: on the contrary it would have set the final seal on my defeat. My salvation was bound up with that of my country as a whole.' Only action could allow a means of transcending the common situation.

When Sartre returned in March 1941 from his period of imprisonment, he was determined to engage on a course of action, to organize a resistance movement of some kind instantly. Simone, for all her agreement, was more sceptical than he, more locked in the sense of impotence which came from living in a Paris under siege where news was censored, where daily one could discover that one's closest friends had suddenly become collaborators. A prisoner-of-war camp had the single advantage of instilling a sense of solidarity amongst the inmates, whereas in Paris, Simone's experience was one of isolation.

Against the odds, a preliminary grouping was formed under the banner of 'Socialism and Liberty'. Composed of writers and intellectuals, its short-term task was to collect and disseminate information. More importantly, by pooling ideas, discussion and research, the group hoped to arrive at some form of left programme for the future. As Sartre explained in his first news bulletin, if Germany won the war, the task would be to see that she lost the peace. In order to widen the support for the group amongst intellectuals of the Free Zone, Sartre and Beauvoir clandestinely crossed the border and spent the summer of 1941 cycling from village to town making contacts.

Their mission met with little success, as indeed did the entire project of 'Socialism and Liberty'. Active resistance work inside France was led by the Communists, whose well-disciplined party machine enabled them to organize effective action. They were suspicious of Sartre and Beauvoir in part because they had not joined the Party before the war despite certain sympathies with its ultimate aim of overthrowing an oppressive bourgeoisie; in part, too, because rumour had it that Sartre's release from the prisoner-of-war camp had been the result of collaborationist intervention. It could only mean that he had agreed to work for the Germans as an *agent collaborateur.*

On their side, Sartre and more particularly Beauvoir, though prepared to work with the Communists, were not prepared to throw in their lot with them altogether. Their attitude to the Communist Party, like that of many left-thinking intellectuals, remained an ambivalent one well into the post-war period. They would not accept that the Party line could dictate to them, particularly on intellectual matters. Nor could they approve Stalin's foreign or internal policy. They remained individualists, or from the Party's viewpoint, *petit-bourgeois* intellectuals. Yet as a result of their successful organization of the Resistence, the Communists in France constituted the largest single left grouping. They were a force to be reckoned with. On several occasions Sartre was ready to join them. Simone, less able to forget personal matters, like the Party's shoddy treatment of their friend Paul Nizan, was never seriously tempted. This political dance of two steps towards the Communist Party, two steps back is one of the themes of her post-war novel, *The Mandarins.*

With 'Socialism and Liberty' disbanded, in part because German reprisals against resistance had now become so severe that Sartre was unwilling to risk lives for an organization like his which had little real effect, Simone and he returned to the one form of resistance work open to them: writing. Only in 1943, when there was real hope that fascism would be defeated, was Sartre invited to engage in the Communist-led Comité National des Ecrivains, the intelligentsia's Resistance grouping. The invitation was not extended to Simone until later that year when *She Came to Stay* at last appeared after various revisions suggested by the publisher (including the exclusion of her first chapters which contained scenes of childhood masturbation). Simone did not accept the invitation, both because she was shy of committees and because she felt that her presence would be superfluous. Sartre, with whom she discussed everything in detail, would already contribute everything that she could. The members of the CNE and their associates, after the Liberation, were to become the key figures of the post-war left intelligentsia.

One of the things it is often hardest to imagine about the war years in Paris is that life effectively went on 'as normal' for long stretches of time. True, all manner of food and basic commodities were in short supply and severe rationing engendered an active black market. This was one of the rare periods in her life, Beauvoir remembers, when she actually cooked and ate at home. True, in the ignorance and isolation from the rest of the world which censorship enforced, people experienced extreme fluctuations of fear and hope as rumours filtered through telling of victories and defeats. But life for the civilian continued. Work was a necessity. Cafés, cinemas, theatres were open, though restricted in what they could show – but not all that restricted, since there were always ways of duping the censors. Simone regularly saw her and Sartre's small circle of friends – their *family* – and made others, Giacometti, Picasso, Adamov, Marcel Camus, Michel Leiris.

For Simone, once she had finished her first published novel, it proved to be one of the most prolific phases of her life. When *The Blood of Others*, the novel she engaged on next, was finally published in 1945 after the Liberation of Paris, it was acclaimed as the great existentialist novel of the Resistance. She wrote a philosophical essay, *Pyrrhus and Cinéas* and began another novel, *All Men are Mortal*. In 1943 Sartre's reputation took a turn for the better. He signed a contract with Pathé to do a series of scenarios. His play, *The Flies*, was staged by a leading director of the pre-war period. *No Exit* was soon to follow. His vast philosophical opus *Being and Nothingness* was published as was a fragment from *The Age of Reason*, part one of his trilogy *Les Chemins de la Liberté*. This, together with the appearance of Beauvoir's first novel and articles by them both in the underground Resistance newspaper, *Combat*, run by the writer Albert Camus, meant that both Sartre and Simone had attained a place to be reckoned with in the French intellectual world. Existentialism, a name coined in fact by the philospher Gabriel Marcel, and not by Sartre, for the set of ideas which Sartre's and Beauvoir's work embodied, was launched. By the end of the war it had taken on such currency that Sartre and Simone suddenly found themselves in the role of public figures.

The spectacle of a philosophy effectively engendering what could without exaggeration be called the first post-war youth movement is a remarkable one. What was it about existentialism that could transform a difficult philosophical system with its roots in the German phenomenological tradition of Husserl and Heidegger, as well as in Kierkegaard, into a life style, a popular religion, a word which encapsulated everything from the moral and political torments of idealistic youth to the latest fashion in clothes, hairdos, song and dance?

The first point to be made about the extraordinary resonance of existentialism is that it presented a war-torn and divided France with a new morality – a set of values which were predicated on a rejection of all previous assumptions. Existentialism fed off the euphoria of liberation. Here was a possibility of saying goodbye to the tawdry recent history of collaboration from which the young wanted, above all else, to dissociate themselves. A new era had begun. Man might no longer be the great hero; the universe might be a senseless void, but despite all that, there was the hope of creating meaning through the struggle for liberty.

On the simplest level, existentialism defined a morality. How do we live? We refuse and consciously question all conventional norms and accepted values, the strictures of society and state. Salvation will come neither from divine quarters nor from any ready-made ideology. Anxiety may result from this recognition for it places responsibility for life totally in human hands; but we must assume this responsibility by exercising our freedom. 'Man,' Beauvoir writes in *The Ethics of Ambiguity* in 1947, 'is neither a stone nor a plant and he cannot complacently justify himself by his mere presence in the world. Man is man only by his refusal to remain passive, by the drive which projects him from the present towards the future and directs him towards things for the purpose of dominating and shaping them. For man, to exist means to remake existence. To live is the will to live.'

Existentialism opened the doors of possibility wiping the tarnished slate of the past for post-war youth. What distinguishes man from the animals, what breaks the cycle of meaningless biological repetition, is the struggle to invent and shape the future. Aspiration and activity define us and free us, though this freedom can only be maintained through a perpetual struggle towards further freedoms.

Man is free: but his freedom is only real and concrete in the measure to which it is engaged – only if it tends towards a goal and works to realize some change in the world. It is by his project in the world that man fully realizes himself ... Man is only free if he gives himself a concrete goal and works to realize it: but a goal can only be a real goal if it is freely chosen.

Neither Sartre nor Beauvoir suggested that the struggle for freedom was easy. Existentialism is haunted by a mood of pessimism, so clearly reflected in the songs of the post-war era. Life is meaningless. It can only be wrested into meaning by action. The human condition, as Beauvoir writes in the Introduction to *The Ethics of Ambiguity*, is a paradoxical one. Man is an animal born to die, but he is also a unique and individual conscious being with aspirations. That consciousness, however, is isolated, an individual subject only to itself in a world of others. Within the collectivity upon which man depends, he is merely an object, a single blade of grass amongst millions.

With the memory of the atrocities of the war still fresh, Beauvoir underlines the fact that people today are more than ever aware of the ambiguity of their condition.

They recognize themselves as the supreme goal towards which all action must be subordinated: but the exigencies of action lead them to treat one another as obstacles or means. The greater their hold over the world, the more they find themselves the victims of uncontrollable forces: masters of the atomic bomb, it is nonetheless created only to destroy them . . . Perhaps in no other epoch have men more brilliantly manifested their greatness, and in no other has this greatness been so atrociously flouted.

It is in the midst of these contradictions that existentialist morality proclaims the need for authenticity in human actions – actions undistorted by dictated duties to state and family – and based on responsible and self-conscious individual choice. The primary existentialist injunction has it that we must recognize the horror of our general condition and particular situation and transcend these by taking responsibilty for our freedom. Difficult enough, this struggle for individual freedom must at all points also take into account the freedom of others. To deny others this struggle is to oppress them. To reject this struggle for oneself, to flee from the anguish of choice and to fall back into a subjection to given conditions is to lapse into bad faith – the cardinal sin in the existentialist universe.

Unlike Sartre, who articulated a developed philosophical system, Simone de Beauvoir only wrote two essays and a handful of articles on existentialism. But her fiction gives a human reality to the philosophy and probes the dilemmas confronted by individuals in their attempt to make moral choices. Already in *She Came to Stay*, the problem of self and other was central – but here the resolution was one of unmitigated individualism. Françoise, the heroine, in order to consolidate her own freedom murders Xavière, that other who limits her freedom.

In *Blood of Others*, written out of the experience of wartime France, Beauvoir casts the problem into a moral and political form – one which fully takes into account the fact that people are at once social beings and individuals.

Jean Blomart is the quintessential existentialist hero. Born into a wealthy printing family, he rebels against privilege and becomes a writer in a rival firm and a trade union leader. But his politics result in the death of an admiring young friend in a political brawl and Jean retreats into a solitary existence, passively refusing emotional and political engagement. The death of his friend has made him feel that all choice is arbitrary, all action, whether romantic or political, which involves one in shaping another's life is both absurd and a curtailment of the other's freedom. He cannot formulate a moral code which does justice to all men. Finally, however, the fact of war and the German Occupation forces him into commitment: he becomes a Resistance leader who organizes guerrilla activity: 'I've learned from this war that there's as much guilt in sparing blood as in shedding it . . . Think of all those lives which our resistance will perhaps save.'

The novel opens with Blomart at the bedside of his lover,

Simone in her mother's flat in 1954, the year she won the Prix
Goncourt

Baby Simone with parents and
extended family (1908), left to
right: father, grandfather, aunt,
mother, uncle

Simone, the teacher, in 1937 at
the Lycée Molière

Simone (right) at eighteen, with her sister Hélène

With her mother in 1954

Making a radio broadcast, 1945

With Jean-Paul Sartre in China, 1955

With Jean-Paul Sartre and
Fidel Castro, Cuba, 1960

In Russia with Sartre and
Krushchev, 1963

Working with Sartre, 1965

Selling *La Cause du Peuple*, 1970

Marching for abortion, Paris 1971

At home, 1975

With Sartre at his flat, 1978

Comforted by her
sister at the funeral
of Jean-Paul Sartre,
19 April 1980

Supported by Lanzmann (right) at Sartre's funeral

Hélène, who has been fatally injured while carrying out a Resistance mission on his instructions. Because of Blomart's decision to act, an innocent person has been killed. This problem was one which haunted Sartre and Simone in the days of Socialism and Liberty and throughout the war. Hélène, the heroine of the novel, solves the moral dilemma for Blomart. With her dying breath, she proclaims her own freedom of choice: it was she who decided to act; she who, in this sense, willed her own death. Blomart's conscience is not at peace, yet he is prepared to continue the struggle for freedom. As Beauvoir notes in her autobiography, the genuinely moral person can never have an easy conscience: liberty is pledged in fear and trembling. Blomart, at Hélène's death bed, reflects to himself, 'If only I dedicate myself to defend the supreme good ... Freedom – then my passion will not have been in vain. You have not given me peace; but why should I desire peace? You have given me the courage to accept forever the risk and the anguish, to bear my crimes and my guilt which will rend me eternally. There is no other way.'

Despite its occasional descent into melodrama and a didacticism which Beauvoir herself was later to criticize severely, the novel is highly readable and fast moving. When it appeared, it had an enormous success. This was not the case for her single attempt at writing for the stage, where Sartre met with such success. *Les bouches inutiles* (*Useless Mouths*) took its title from the name given in Italian city-states to those women, children and old people who, in order to stave off famine during a siege, were executed. The play's theme is similar to that of her resistance novel. Has one the right to sacrifice individuals for the general future good? Clumsily constructed, sententious to a fault, the political currency of Beauvoir's single play did nothing to save it from a short stage life.

The reading which led Simone to *Les bouches inutiles* was, in fact, background for her next novel, *All Men are Mortal*. She saw the book as a complement to *She Came to Stay* and as the antithesis of *The Blood of Others*. In some ways her most ambitious fiction, *All Men are Mortal* is also Beauvoir's grandest failure. Her wartime obsession with history and her reading of Hegel find expression here in a purely imaginative work. Set in part in the late Middle Ages and the sixteenth century, in part in occupied France, the novel has as its hero Fosca who drinks an elixir of immortality in order to survive the siege of his native Carmona which he wants so much to liberate from the oppressor. His stubborn success not only costs countless lives, but leaves Italy divided and defenceless against foreign invasion. Then, as adviser to the Emperor Charles V, Fosca seeks to unite the world – a goal the achievement of which will, he thinks, bring to an end the mutability of history. Terrible massacres ensue and Fosca realizes that his quest for an absolute good is doomed. Men are divided against one another. They do not want ultimate happiness. They only want to live. Where Blomart suffered from his belief that he was responsible for everything, where Françoise had wanted to do everything, Fosca's experience leads him to feel that nothing can be done. He, as an individual, can do nothing. Beauvoir points to the idea that although collectively people can achieve much, no single and absolute vision like Fosca's can be imposed on a multifarious world. In her autobiography she explains that through this fiction she also wanted to attack the Communists' notion of a monolithic Humanity caught in the march of History.

Fosca tells his story to Régine, the proud and ambitious woman who wants his love because, through it, she will achieve an absolute and incontestable uniqueness. To be at the centre of an immortal's gaze is, for her, once and for all to transcend the humiliation of the image others have of one. With horror, Régine realizes that precisely the opposite has happened.

Rich in ambiguities and narrative potential, *All Men are Mortal* yet falls between fable, romance and historical narrative without ever quite finding a consistent voice. Its appearance marked the end of the first phase of Beauvoir's fiction in which philosophical and moral problems gave shape to narrative and dramatic development.

The end of the war found Simone de Beauvoir and Sartre no longer on the sidelines aspiring to be writers but at the very centre of French intellectual, literary and political life. In the 'orgy of brotherhood' which followed upon German defeat, it seemed an easy step to move from Resistance to socialism and radically to remake social structures without precipitating any new convulsions. Socialist and communist principles had always been close to Sartre and Beauvoir's left anarchism, but before the war they had conceived of them as constituting a threat to their individuality. Now socialism appeared as humanity's only hope for instituting the democratic principles in which they believed.

The men now in power had been in the Resistance and, to a greater or lesser extent, we knew them all. We could count many of the important figures in the press and radio as close friends. Politics had become a family matter and we expected to have a hand in it. 'Politics is no longer dissociated from individuals,' Camus wrote in *Combat* ... 'it is man's direct address to other men.' We were writers, and that was our job, to address ourselves to other men. Before the war, few intellectuals had tried to understand their epoch; all – or almost all – had failed in the attempt ... It was our turn to carry the torch.

One of the ways in which the torch could be carried was to found a magazine. *Les Temps Modernes* (*Modern Times*) was born in late 1944. The editorial committee included Sartre and Beauvoir, Maurice Merleau-Ponty, who became the editor-in-chief and political director; the philosopher Raymond Aron, Sartre's old school friend who had just returned from Free France headquarters in London and was acting as adviser to André Malraux, the Minister of Information; and one of the three directors of the newspaper *Combat*. Simone was delegated to obtain paper, still in short supply, from the Ministry of Information and she recounts with glee how she managed to convince the relevant official of the importance of the project. The first issue of *Les Temps Modernes* appeared on 15 October 1945. The review was to remain at the centre of French intellectual life for the next twenty-five years, taking up radical and left-wing positions on the home and the international front. Many of Beauvoir's post-war writings, including chapters from *The Second Sex*, first appeared here.

The magazine's early history was characterized by splits in the editorial committee. At first Sartre thought it would be possible to work with the Communists, the largest single grouping on the left and the only one to have a working-class base, and still maintain independence; but as revelations about Stalin's labour camps filtered through to the West and the Cold War loomed, this proved impossible. Sartre was once again attacked by the Communist Party for catering to the young, for his links with 'the Nazi philosopher Heidegger', for his wartime theatrical work in a theatre which excluded Jews. All this Simone incorporated into her most important novel, *The Mandarins*.

With the establishment of *Les Temps Modernes* the existentialist vogue reached its height. Sartre and Beauvoir, at first unwilling to accept the journalistic tag given to them, finally had little choice but to acquiesce. Articles attacking or applauding them filled the press. They lectured to vast audiences: during Sartre's famous 'Existentialism is a Humanism' lecture, women fainted, people burst into cheers or heckled angrily. Existentialist black sweaters and existentialist long straight hair and pale faces became the fashionable garb to be worn in left-bank cafés and existentialist dives where Juliette Greco sang existentialist songs and young people performed wild boogie-woogies or sat in angst-ridden solitude staring into glasses. *Life* Magazine carried a spread on existentialism and suddenly cafés and dives were full of tourists. The movement spread to America. Sartre was crowned the pope of existentialism and Simone acclaimed as Notre-Dame-de-Sartre, Our Lady of Sartre. At once idol of the young and the Catholic press's favourite dissolute madwoman, champion of free love and purveyor of a host of vices, Simone, in fact, carried on life as usual.

She still inhabited hotel rooms, read and wrote daily and frequented her favourite cafés and clubs where an extended circle of friends now met. The only significant change which fame brought was that she stopped teaching altogether – despite the fact that the University now saw fit to reinstate her. For a brief time she became financially dependent on Sartre.

'I have so often advised women to be independent and said that independence begins in the purse, that I feel I must explain this attitude which at the time seemed to speak for itself,' she writes in her autobiography. In reality, since she could always go back to teaching, her financial autonomy was assured. Moreover, her writing had become a demanding task – one which 'guaranteed my moral autonomy; in the solitude of risks taken, of decisions to be made, I made my freedom much more real than by accommodating myself to any money-making routine'. There was so much to do: novels, essays, articles to be written, a reportage trip to Portugal to make and very soon a whole new area of research to be undertaken, for a further aspect of the human condition had begun to interest Simone.

The war had made Simone aware of what she shared with other women. It had also illuminated her about a difference. During 1944, she had begun to meet a new set of women of her own age, most of whom, unlike her close circle, led ordinary married lives. They 'had all undergone an identical experience: they had lived as "dependent persons"'. These women had begun to talk to Simone about things she had never considered. 'I began to take stock of the difficulties, deceptive advantages, traps and manifold obstacles that most women encounter in their path. I also felt how much they were both diminished and enriched by this experience.' The seeds of *The Second Sex* were sown. Perhaps no other single book in the twentieth century has had quite such an impact on individual consciousness and those very social conditions Beauvoir now saw as the writer's task to transform.

FIVE

Being a Woman

As she approached her fortieth birthday, Simone de Beauvoir began increasingly to be preoccupied by the question, 'What has it meant to me to be a woman?' Concerned to emphasize that her own intellectual and authorial voice was not a marginal one – one specific to her place as a woman – Beauvoir was always fierce in her declarations that within her own circle she was treated and acted as an 'equal', indeed a privileged equal; and that the question of her femininity rarely came into play: 'I had never had any feeling of inferiority, no one had ever said to me: "You think that way because you're a woman"; my femininity had never been irksome to me in any way.' Beauvoir was explicitly not a feminist. Yet when she sat down to the task of writing about herself, the question of her womanhood suddenly took primary place. 'Wanting to talk about myself, I became aware that to do so I should first have to describe the condition of women in general.' Sartre encouraged her to look into the matter further. 'I looked and it was a revelation: the world was a masculine world, my childhood had been nourished by myths formed by men, and I hadn't reacted to them in at all the same way I should have done if I had been a boy.'

Despite the 'objective' philosophical tone it adopts, *The Second Sex* is in many ways one of Beauvoir's most personal books. The cumulative anger and humiliation which are part of the tone of the text, whatever the calm authority of its statements, have spoken intimately to generations of women and forcefully illuminated the confusions and frustrations we experience. It is not insignificant that Beauvoir wrote the book during the most passionate of her 'contingent' love affairs and the one which most seriously threatened her relationship with Sartre. Neither is it altogether coincidental that her interest in women's condition should surface just at the time that Sartre was deeply involved with another woman. This lends a certain poignancy to the sections of the book which deal with women in love.

In this most influential of her books Beauvoir exposes femininity as a cultural construct, systematically analyses the contradictions underlying the notion of femininity and attacks the feminine mystique. In accordance with the lessons the war taught her, Beauvoir describes the fortunes of the individual in terms of liberty and not in terms of happiness. She is ruthlessly honest in charting woman's marginality, her historic and cultural exclusion from the term 'man'. Nor is she afraid to expose woman's complicity in the making and sustaining of her condition. And Beauvoir is concerned to show that it is a *condition*, not an essential fact. Thus woman's state clearly emerges as something which can be changed. 'One is not born, but rather becomes, a woman. No biological, psychological or economic fate determines the figure that the human female presents in society; it is civilization as a whole that produces this

87

creature, intermediate between male and eunuch, which is described as feminine.'

Beauvoir's vantage point is that of existentialist philosophy: to look reality squarely and honestly in the face and having done so to assume the responsibility of changing it by engaging in a struggle for freedom. We can look at the problems this poses in a moment, but first of all it is important to see the advantages such existentialist thinking contributes to her analysis. Principal amongst these is the idea of the Other. In Beauvoir's definition, the state woman inhabits in our world is that of the 'looked at', the Other, the oppressed consciousness, the object who is always seen by men and is thus perpetually denied subjecthood.

... humanity is male and man defines woman not in herself but as relative to him; she is not regarded as an autonomous being ... For him she is sex, absolute sex, no less. She is defined and differentiated with reference to man and not he with reference to her; she is the incidental, the inessential as opposed to the essential. He is the Subject, he is the Absolute – she is the Other.

How has this state of affairs come about? Though she claims that she rejects any form of determinism, including the biological, Beauvoir's explanation in part contradicts this. In elucidating why this is a man's world, she looks to early societies and there finds that 'the bondage of reproduction was a terrible handicap in the struggle against a hostile world'.

According to her Hegelian analysis wherever there are two human categories, each aspires to impose its sovereignty over the other. If both are equal, a reciprocal relation results. If one of the two is more privileged, has some advantage, then this one will prevail over the other. Women's disadvantage is that 'pregnancy, childbirth and menstruation reduced their capacity for work and made them at times wholly dependent upon the men for protection and food'. Locked in a process of repetition of natural functions, imprisoned in the bodily cycle of life itself, woman, like an animal, produced nothing new, whereas man transcended mere 'life', invented tools and created values which deprived pure repetition of all value. Man's activity prevailed over the confused forces of life, subdued nature and woman, and shaped the future. Men became the masters of value against which women, the Other, were defined.

Beauvoir's scrutiny of history, myth and literature reveals how the fundamental hidden assumption in all culture is that the masculine is the absolute human type against which woman is measured and defined. A whole series of oppositions evolve from the basic duality of Subject and Other, masculine and feminine which Beauvoir posits. Where the masculine is culture, the feminine is nature, where he is human, she is animal, and so on through. intellect/instinct rational/irrational, activity/-passivity, production/reproduction. Though occasionally idealized, the second term is never the dominant one, never the source of absolute value. Woman emerges as the container of man's otherness, his own inevitable alienation. Whereas in defining his humanity, man creates, invents and hurls himself towards a freely chosen future, woman, bound by the immanence of reproduction, is denied her own humanity.

Dependent and Other, woman is nonetheless a necessity

to man. In the Hegelian dualism of Beauvoir's system, the master could not survive without the slave:

In woman is incarnated in positive form the lack that the existent [male] carries in his heart, and it is in seeking to be made whole through her that man hopes to attain self-realization . . . Treasure, prey, sport and danger, nurse, guide, judge, mediatrix, mirror, woman is the Other in whom the subject transcends himself without being hunted, who opposes him without denying him; she is the other who lets herself be taken without ceasing to be the other, and therein she is so necessary to man's happiness and to his triumph that it can be said that if she did not exist, men would have invented her.

As Other, woman comes to represent everything that man desires and wants to tame. Yet she exists apart from men's desires and she cannot be permanently tamed, despite cultural forces, social regulations and the whole repertoire of religious and superstitious dogma: '. . . she is not only the incarnation of their dream, but also its frustration'. The fact of this frustration accounts for the retinue of misogynist characteristics attributed to women. 'When she falls from the ideal in which man has placed her, woman is exposed as mediocre and false.'

Beauvoir urges women to assume their status as subjects, to become independent, the active makers of their own destiny. She recognizes that even at a time when control over reproduction is possible and when some progress has been made towards equality, for women to transcend their condition is not a simple matter. Men are still in power everywhere.

To decline to be the Other, to refuse to be a party to the deal – this would be for women to renounce all the advantages conferred upon them by their alliance with the superior caste. Man-the-sovereign will provide woman-the-liege with material protection and will undertake the moral justification of her existence; thus she can evade at once both economic risk and the metaphysical risk of a liberty in which ends and aims must be contrived without assistance.

It is easier, Beauvoir states, to be complicit. Yet to accept the status of Otherness, is to accept an inauthentic existence, to allow oneself to become a thing, 'passive, lost, ruined'.

In Book Two of *The Second Sex*, originally published some months after Book One, Beauvoir anatomizes 'woman's life today' from cradle to grave. She shows how little girls who originally assume their equality with boys are moulded into those 'wounded, shameful, culpable' creatures who cannot become 'grown up' without accepting a feminine sexuality which condemns them to a mutilated and fixed existence. She traces the conflicts and contradictions which attend an adolescence spent in waiting for a man. With an honesty which shocked her contemporaries, Beauvoir explores sexual initiation and female eroticism, showing how taboos, prohibitions and prejudices all work against the young woman's enjoyment of her own sexuality. Turning her rigorous gaze to marriage, Beauvoir attacks an institution which oppresses and torments both its partners. She makes an impassioned plea for the transformation of marriage which means, in effect, transforming the condition of women in general, for only when women are free, when women can rely on themselves, will men be free.

In her chapter on motherhood, Beauvoir broaches what

in the 1940s was forbidden territory: abortion. She exposes Catholic hypocrisy which condemns abortion because unborn children cannot be baptized and thus accepted into Heaven, and the social hypocrisy which permits the middle-class woman to have a 'therapeutic' abortion and calls the working-class woman's abortion a crime. Contraception and abortion, Beauvoir argues, would permit women to undertake their maternities in freedom, something which could only benefit both mother and child. Always a critic of the mindless drudgery to which maternity condemned women, Beauvoir was also keenly aware that idealized motherhood was a cultural myth invented by men. Here she attacks the assumption that maternity is necessarily the culmination of woman's life: 'It is . . . deceptive to dream of gaining through the child a plenitude, a warmth, a value, which one is unable to create for oneself . . . no more than any other enterprise does it represent a ready-made justification.'

What is equally deceptive is for women to attempt to attain transcendence from within their prison of immanence. The walls of the prison must first be broken down. Only the collective struggle for liberation, first and foremost on an economic plane, will alter women's condition. But many women, Beauvoir points out, attempt to achieve salvation by solitary effort. They find justification for their existence by painting their servitude in the colours of freedom. This false consciousness is the fate of the narcissist, the mystic and the woman in love – prime and typical examples of the mutilation women suffer in their condition as Other.

These three case studies of Beauvoir's contain some of her most brilliant analysis of woman's condition. In 'The Narcissist' she describes that kind of woman who takes herself as the object of her own love and desires. For a being who is already Other and cannot fufil herself through projects in the external world, this is an easy rut to slip into.

A man who acts must necessarily size himself up. Ineffective, isolated, woman can neither find her place nor take her own measure; she gives herself supreme importance because no object of importance is accessible to her ... Her education has prompted her to identify herself with her own body, puberty has revealed this body as being passive and desirable; it is something she can touch, like satin or velvet, and can contemplate with a lover's eye. In solitary pleasure, woman may divide herself into male subject and female object ...

But this duality is only a dream; there can be no real relation between an individual and her double and as age takes its toll, frustrations accrue. In her struggle to gain that approval from others essential to her vanity, but ever more difficult to acquire with age, the narcissist grows over-sensitive, irritable, paranoid. The illusion of narcissistic independence is shattered to reveal a total and slavish dependence.

Beauvoir's portraits of the woman in love and the mystic have particular bite, perhaps because they most closely bear the traces of her own experience. She begins her chapter on the woman in love by pointing out the different weight men and women attach to love; for man, the active sovereign subject, woman is one value amongst many; for woman, man is the absolute through whom she believes she achieves her transcendence. While being the most attractive path for woman to embark on, love is also her greatest trap. From childhood on everything in society conspires to make woman believe that her salvation lies in love. And indeed, for a while, 'the woman in love is endowed with a high and undeniable value'. Yet, in time, the chosen idol is revealed not to be God and searing disappointment ensues. From the superhuman, the man becomes inhuman: the woman in love judges her judge with utmost severity and ends by denying him his liberty so that he may deserve to remain her master. Since her devotion and service is absolute, so must his superiority and his attention to her be. And yet if he spends all his time with her, focuses only on her, he is robbed of his freedom and is no longer the god she wishes to serve. In this paradox, lie the many pitfalls of the woman in love, for whom jealousy is a constant stalking partner, 'There are few crimes that entail worse punishment than the generous fault of putting oneself entirely in another's hands,' Beauvoir writes.

It is a brief step from adoring the god in man to adoring God Himself. The psychological and sexual constellation which shapes the woman in love is parallel to that of the mystic. The loved one, man or God, is always more or less absent. She gives herself to him through an act of faith. Whether she loves the god she makes of man or God Himself, woman continues to live on her knees.

Beauvoir's fierce indictment of women's narcissism, desire for absolute love and mysticism are based on her understanding of these as a flight from freedom and transcendence. The only way that woman can employ her liberty authentically is to project it through positive action into human society. It is only when she is productive, active, engages on projects in the world that woman acquires the status of a subject. Beauvoir advocates the path of independence. She does not, however, minimize its difficulties. Rereading the last sections of *The Second Sex*, I am struck by how apposite her comments still are, some forty years after the publication of this pioneering book, years which have seen the burgeoning of the women's movement.

Beauvoir describes how the independent woman is still prey to the contradictions of her sexual and emotional life. Man enjoys the advantage that, from his childhood on, his vocation as a human being runs parallel to his destiny as a male. He is not divided against himself. Yet woman, in order to realize her femininity, her sexuality, must make herself both object and prey.

She refuses to confine herself to her role as female, because she will not accept mutilation; but it would also be a mutilation to repudiate her sex. Man is a human being with sexuality; woman is a complete individual, equal to the male, only if she too is a human being with sexuality. To renounce her femininity is to renounce a part of her humanity.

This conflict which is fundamental to women in our culture makes relations with men particularly problematic. Brought up to see an idealization of the male as fundamental to love, how is the independent woman to prevent herself from falling on her knees and losing herself in her loved one; or conversely how is she to find erotic fulfilment with a man she considers an equal and not a superior?

Maternity poses a further problem: how is the independent

working woman to meet the demands of motherhood and what still remains her domain of responsibility, the home? Beauvoir points out that 'the independent woman of today is torn between her professional interests and the problems of her sexual life; it is difficult for her to strike a balance between the two; if she does, it is at the price of concessions and sacrifices which require her to be in a constant state of tension'. This tension, the contradictory demands and expectations placed on women both by society and themselves, is in large part responsible for the various discomforts and illnesses which women suffer.

It is clear from *The Second Sex* that woman's condition will not change unless there is concerted action both by men and women towards radical social transformation. The book ends with a quote from Karl Marx: 'The direct, natural, necessary relation of human creatures is the relation of man to woman.' Only when we abolish the slavery of half of humanity can the reign of liberty be established.

Yet Beauvoir's hope here seems to rest on the individual woman's struggle toward independence and, particularly, the middle-class woman with professional aspirations. As many feminists have recently argued, Beauvoir's analysis of woman's condition and particularly the strategy she defines for independence are open to criticism.

There is no doubt that *The Second Sex* is embued with the self-same masculine bias that Beauvoir attacks as having created women's condition. In her positing of the Manichean dualities which emerge from the basic opposition of self and Other, masculine and feminine, it is to the first term, the male, that she invariably attributes the greater value.

'Rationality', 'objectivity' are her preferred home ground and she universalizes their potential good without scrutinizing them in any detail. As I have said *The Second Sex* is in many ways an intensely personal book and Beauvoir projects her own rational proclivity, her admiration for the generalizing intellect into the entirety of her analysis. She fails to see any 'good' in those characteristics which she attributes to the feminine. Unlike later feminists, she sees little that is potentially positive in the very particularities of women's separate experience which she describes. For her, sexuality, maternity are always prisons, the menopause a release. Nor does Beauvoir see any limitations in the male perspective. Yet activity may not always be a virtue over passivity. The man, too, may not always be at home with his body and its sexuality. Her own stringent dualism prevents her from seeing the slippages between her terms which are part of daily experience for both women and men. As Margaret Walters points out, Beauvoir attacks the mystique of femininity only to end up by accepting a masculine mystique.

This is nowhere clearer than in her portrayal of the independent woman:

The emancipated woman wants to be active, a taker, and refuses the passivity man means to impose on her. The 'modern' woman accepts masculine values; she prides herself in thinking, taking action, working, creating on the same terms as man.

What then is to become of those areas of women's experience which, as Beauvoir herself underlines, are different – sexuality, childbearing, motherhood?

Part of the problem lies in the very nature of Beauvoir's existentialist ethic. To make of freedom and the individual's freely chosen project in the world the ultimate good is both to turn a blind eye to the many possible constraints on freedom and to suggest that the liberal capitalist male – the successful self-made man who has a veneer of social concern – is the ideal human type. During the war, Beauvoir had argued with Sartre that not every individual's situation would permit an equally active transcendence of their context. She had given the example of a woman in a harem. 'I stuck to my point for a long time,' she writes, 'and in the end made only a token submission. Basically I was right. But to defend my attitude I should have had to abandon the place of individual, and therefore idealistic, morality on which we had set ourselves.'

In writing *The Second Sex* Beauvoir is still loathe to abandon this idealistic morality. She makes a few token gestures away from it by suggesting that the working-class woman may not find in labour the transcendence that the professional woman does, or that the shop girl may prefer marriage to the drudgery and emptiness of work. Summarily, she states that in these cases independence can only be achieved when the class as a whole is free from oppression. But her main focus remains the individual and hence the middle-class professional woman. Her idealistic insistence on freedom also blinds her in part to the uses both dialectical materialism and psychoanalysis could have been put to in her analysis of woman's condition. In *Force of Circumstance*, the third volume of her autobiography, she states that if she were to rewrite *The Second Sex* now, she would take a more materialist position. She would base 'the notion of woman as Other and the Manichean argument it entails not on an idealistic and *a priori* struggle of consciences, but on the facts of supply and demand'. She also states, 'I never cherished any illusion of changing woman's condition; it depends on the future of Labour in the world; it will change significantly only at the price of a revolution in production.'

Yet during the time that she writes *The Second Sex* Beauvoir is inherently opposed to what she construes as the determinism both of dialectical materialism and psychoanalysis. Her existentialist liberalism ultimately refuses any limits to freedom – an understanding that choices can be made freely and yet be bound by constraints and circumstances not within the individual's own power. As her chapters on historical materialism and psychoanalysis in *The Second Sex* make clear, her thinking here is somewhat superficial. Psychoanalysis, particularly, was to remain an intellectual bugbear for many years, perhaps because Beauvoir defended herself so assiduously against the possibility that unconscious and ungovernable fantasies could exist which could shape her own actions without her conscious knowledge. Beauvoir's personal strengths – the force of her unflinching hold on the rational, her stubborn self-determination – are the values she projects into her analysis of women's condition and the means to its transcendence.

This said, and with all its slightly anachronistic biology and anthropology, *The Second Sex* remains an encyclopedic *tour de force*, a formidable pioneering study of the social, economic, historical and psychological determinants of woman's condition. It is the one book that could be said to have set the agenda for the woman's movement. No other analysis of the feminine mystique has so fully and so subtly investigated the cultural factors which shape women's experience and their situation in the world. Millions of copies of the books have been read and continue to be read worldwide, while women's studies courses explore the terrain Beauvoir so effectively mapped out.

Neither must Beauvoir's bravery be forgotten, her bold frankness in broaching topics which had rarely found a public outside clinical circles. Female sexuality, masturbation, lesbianism, menstruation and the like were hardly topics of everyday discourse. Indeed, when *The Second Sex* first appeared in a France still deeply Catholic and moving towards the conservatism of the 1950s, it caused a veritable furore. Twenty-two thousand copies of the first volume were sold in the first week and the second volume, as well as the relevant issues of *Les Temps Modernes*, were brought up like hot cakes. The scandal the book provoked, much to Simone's surprise, was as great as its success.

I received – some signed and some anonymous – epigrams, epistles, satires, admonitions, and exhortations addressed to me by, for example, 'some very active members of the First Sex'. Unsatisfied, frigid, priapic, nymphomaniac, lesbian, a hundred times aborted, I was everything, even an unmarried mother.

The Catholic novelist, François Mauriac, wrote to one of the contributors to *Les Temps Modernes* to say: 'Your employer's vagina has no secrets from me.' In the press, Simone was accused of being, in turn, a poor neurotic girl, repressed, frustrated and cheated by life, a virago, a women who'd never properly been made love to, envious, embittered – in fact that entire sequence of epithets we have become accustomed to in reviews of feminist writing over the years. Albert Camus accused her of making the French male look ridiculous. The Church put the book on the black list, while the popular magazine, *Paris Match*, devoted a seven-page feature to Beauvoir. The offices of *Les Temps Modernes* were so besieged by requests for the addresses of abortionists that the secretary put up a poster proclaiming, 'We do it on the premises, ourselves.'

Simone also received countless letters from women all over the world and from various walks of life expressing their debt to her: 'You book was a great help to me. Your book saved me . . .' Her initial response to this was one of surprise. In no way had she suspected the impact her study of woman's condition would have. Indeed, both in *The Second Sex* itself and in her autobiography, there is a residual embarrassment related to the fact that she is writing about and for women – not the primary task of a philosopher. With an authority tinged by a characteristic ambivalence about her own inclusion in the category 'woman', she notes:

I don't regret that it has been so. Divided, lacerated, in a world made to put them at a disadvantage, for women there are far more victories to be won, more prizes to be gained, more defeats to be suffered than there are for men. I have an interest in them: and I prefer having taken a limited but real hold upon the world through them than to drifting in the universal.

During the entirety of the time in which she was engaged in writing *The Second Sex*, the contradictions to do with the 'feminine' side of Simone's life were particularly acute. That mutilation which Beauvoir describes as woman's lot whether she rejects or embraces her sexuality, that division against herself which is the condition of the independent woman, were Simone's own. While Sartre's and her fame spread, making them the existentialist duo *par excellence*, and public lectures and interviews as well as numerous trips followed one upon another in quick succession, their personal union was seriously threatened. Sartre was involved in a passionate affair with a woman he had met in America, a relationship which, unlike the vast run of his conquests since Olga, threw Simone into a state of anxiety. Dolores Vanetti (known in the autobiography as M.) was an actress who had worked in Paris before the war and in the United States had become the mistress of the surrealist writer, André Breton. Sartre had met her there and had instantly returned to see her after only a brief stay in Paris. He had told Simone that he would be spending two to three months a year with Dolores, with whom he was in complete harmony. Nervously Simone asked Sartre who meant more to him, she or Dolores. She means an enormous amount to me, Sartre had replied, 'but I am with you'.

Though this answer partly satisfied Simone, it did not make her life any easier. Sartre was too attached to Dolores to give her up, nor did she want to play the contingent role in his and Simone's necessary love. Sartre had apparently made it clear to Dolores that there could be no question of their living together, but as Beauvoir writes, 'By saying that he loved her he gave the lie to that warning; for – especially in the eyes of women – love triumphs over every obstacle

. . . It was natural for M. to think: " "Things will change".'
Sartre wanted neither to lose Dolores nor Simone, and
during his periods of separation from Dolores, his lobsters
began to reappear. The exigencies of the pact between him
and Simone were taking their toll. Simone, despite her independence and cool self-control, reacted in one of the traditional ways open to women; she engaged in an affair of her
own and in direct parallel to Sartre's, in America.

The United States had always held a special place in
Simone's imagination. She read its fiction avidly, everything
from Faulkner to thrillers, and she translated new writing
for Sartre who didn't have her fluency in English. Both of
them loved Hollywood films, blues and jazz. Then, too, despite
the fact that the United States was the 'homeland of capitalism' which they were opposed to, it had helped save Europe
from Fascism. Enthusiastically in 1947 Simone embarked
on a university lecture tour, talking from coast to coast
about the moral problems of the post-war writer, about
the writer's responsibility and the need for engagement if
another debacle on the scale of World War II was to be
prevented. The *New Yorker* hailed Simone as the 'prettiest
existentialist'; *The New York Times Magazine* commissioned a
piece from her on an existentialist's view of America. Simone
was fêted and made much of. With her customary traveller's
energy, she walked for miles, visited bars and drugstore
counters, made forays into the forbidden world of Harlem –
all of which was to find its place in *America Day By Day*, so
subtle a portrait of her subject, that but for a few historical
changes, her observations remain as fresh as they were in
1947.

Coming from a post-war Paris still poor in basic commodities, where the rifts between collaborators and resisters were slow to heal, she at first experienced America like a breath of fresh air. People were friendly, generous, enthusiastic. She admired their dynamism, their ceaseless activity, their entrepreneurial qualities. Despite all this, however, her account of America is a tersely critical one. Americans were only interested in results, not in the human experience which produced them. Thus the value of all results was reduced to a cash value. As for the countless commodities and infinite possibilities America offered: 'This useless profusion mystifies. Here are a thousand possibilities open to choice: but they are all the same. In this way Americans can enjoy their freedom, subject to conditions imposed upon them, and without ever criticizing that they are not true conditions of freedom.' In America, she writes, the individual is nothing. He is the object of an abstract cult.

American publishers and intellectuals worried her. Publishers talked only of products and markets, despising writers and readers equally. At the offices of the important *Partisan Review*, she was told: 'In France you ask questions, but you do not answer them. But we do not ask them; we answer them.' More frighteningly, there was the situation of the blacks and Simone, adept at unpacking prejudices, is scathing about racism and white hypocrisy. How can the people who are despised, called dirty, be the very same ones who are brought in to rear one's children? Then too, the Cold War atmosphere, the hatred of the left, terrified her. Everywhere she saw the will to a new war. People were not really prepared to hear about the situation in Europe or learn from the European experience. Their attitude to France was underscored by contempt. After all the Marshall Plan was bailing Europe out and Americans were saviours. Beauvoir's comment on the nature of American imperialism is particularly acute: 'In the eyes of the average American, imperialism takes on the guise of charity. Their arrogance lies not in their love of power. It is the love of imposing on others that which is good. The miracle is that the key to paradise should be in their hands.'

Simone's New York acquaintances had suggested that during her brief stay in Chicago she look up the left-wing writer Nelson Algren, whose novel, *The Man With the Golden Arm*, was later to win the Pulitzer Prize. In 1947 Algren's first novel, *Neon Wilderness*, peopled with the drug addicts, criminals and prostitutes he chose to live his life with, had just met with a critical success. Simone had had enough of starched university and ambassadorial dinners and cocktail parties. Algren's Chicago was the America she wanted to see. She rang him up and Algren, unable to understand her staccato and heavily accented voice, hung up twice. But finally they met and in a manner one hardly expects from the demystifying Simone de Beauvoir of *The Second Sex* or of the cool narrator of the autobiography, fell in love. In her novel, *The Mandarins*, where Beauvoir through the character of Anne recounts a barely fictionalized version of their relationship, this first meeting takes on all the moment of a true romance.

I knocked and there appeared at the door a rather tall, rather young man, his chest stiffened by a leather jacket. He looked at me in surprise.

'You found the house?'

'So it seems.'

A black stove was crackling in the middle of a yellow kitchen; old newspapers were scattered about on the linoleum covering the floor, and I noticed there wasn't any refrigerator. With a vague gesture, Brogan pointed to the papers. 'I was trying to clean up a bit.'

'I hope I'm not disturbing you.'

'No, not at all.' He stood in front of me with an embarrassed look on his face.

They talk, learn each other's pasts. They walk through the cold Chicago streets and sit in bars. Then it is time for the Simone character to go.

'Come back,' Brogan said, and quickly, he added, 'I don't want to think that I'm not going to see you again.'

Silently we walked to a hack stand. When he drew his face close to mine I couldn't keep myself from turning my head away, but I felt his breath against my mouth.

In the train a few hours later, while trying to read Brogan's novel, I chided myself severely. 'It's ridiculous! At my age!' But like a virgin's my mouth still tingled. I had never kissed a man except those with whom I had slept; and each time that shadow of a kiss flashed through my mind, it seemed as if I were going to rediscover burning rememberances of love in the deepest recesses of my memory.

What Simone experienced with Algren was a passionate and tumultuous love. Sartre may have been instrumental in its inception by asking Simone to prolong her stay in the US for ten days, since Dolores was still in Paris. It was during this period that the relationship with Algren was consummated. But the continuation of the relationship was all her doing. In Algren Simone had met a man whom she could both talk to as an equal and love erotically, emotionally. Her sexual relations with Sartre had all but ceased around 1944. The relationship with Bost had continued but in a desultory fashion and had never blossomed into passion. Simone's letters to Algren, some 1800 pages of them, bear witness to a passion which lasted for five years. The Simone de Beauvoir visible in them is hardly the severely intellectual companion of Jean-Paul Sartre, but rather a tender, playful, tormented woman in love.

By her own account, after this first trip to America Simone returned to Paris in a dreadful state. She had told Algren, before leaving, that her life was permanently fixed in Paris, but that somehow she would see him again. Like Sartre, but perhaps more tensely poised than he, she was walking a tightrope: at once trying to maintain what to her was a profoundly important working relationship and friendship with Sartre and engaging in a passion which threatened to overwhelm her. Simone wondered whether she ought to give up the latter before it took on more weight. 'I asked myself that question with an anxiety that bordered on mental aberration.' She underwent a severe crisis which, as seemed to have been perennially the case for her, took on physical dimensions. On a recuperative trip to Sweden with Sartre, she suffered from nightmares: 'I can remember a yellow eye at the back of my head which was being pierced by a long knitting needle.'

It is a puzzle why, in the circumstances, she didn't consider leaving Sartre, particularly since he was still deeply entangled with Dolores. But for Beauvoir, their pact was absolute. In her letters to Algren over the next years, her detached perspective on Sartre's Don Juanism is clear: 'He is persuaded that it isn't enough to have a brunette of an Arlette, a blonde Wanda, two artificial blondes, Michel and Evelyne, he needs a redhead too. He finds one in Brazil . . .' Yet she tries to explain to Algren how the work she does with Sartre 'filtering' his book on Jean Genet as she has done for so many other of his books, is crucially important to her. She cannot leave Sartre. Neither can she abandon her own writing, her commitment to her own work. To write in America for any extended period of time, to live there, would be impossible. Her life, her responsibility, lies in France.

Yet Simone returned to Chicago immediately after her trip to Sweden. She and Algren lived together, and worked side-by-side in his two-room flat. He asked her to stay on, to marry him. She refused, returned to the US again in May 1948 and the two of them travelled together down the Mississippi and into Mexico. The trip was cut short by Simone's promise that she would return to Paris in July to help Sartre with a script. Algren was enraged, but again he asked her to stay on. Simone left, only to find on her return to Paris that Sartre had gone down to the South coast with Dolores. At a loose end, Simone rang Algren, but he refused to have her return. They met again the following year in Paris, but despite Simone's desire to have the relationship continue, Algren's patience with Simone's attachment to Sartre was growing thin. Like Dolores, he couldn't understand why, given their love, Simone would neither live with him, nor marry him and have his child. When they met again in 1950, Algren announced that he was about to remarry his first wife. He couldn't love a woman who placed another man before him, a woman whom he could only see for a few weeks a year.

The depth of passion within this relationship, Algren's very real sense of betrayal when it was over, is perhaps best visible in his venomous attack on Beauvoir's *Force of Circumstance* when it appeared in the US in 1965. In this volume of her autobiography, Beauvoir, amidst much else, tersely recounts her affair with Algren and confronts the question of contingent loves, of fidelity and freedom. She does so in the coolly judicious tone which is that of the autobiography as a whole and only hints at the very real anguish present in *The Mandarins*, and, I imagine, in her experience of the events as they were lived in the heat of the moment – not after a twelve-year reflective interval.

Is there any possible reconciliation between fidelity and freedom? And if so, at what price?

Often preached, rarely practised, complete fidelity is usually experienced by those who impose it on themselves as a mutilation; they console themselves for it by sublimations or by drink ... There are many couples who conclude more or less the same pact as Sartre and myself: to maintain throughout all deviations from the main path a 'certain fidelity'. 'I have been faithful to thee, Cynara, in my fashion.' Such an undertaking has its risks. It is always possible, that one of the partners may prefer a new attachment to the old one, the other partner then considering himself unjustly betrayed; in place of two free persons, a victim and a torturer confront each other.

In certain cases, for one reason or another – children, a common concern, the force of the attachment – the couple is impregnable. If the two allies allow themselves only passing sexual liaisons, then there is no difficulty, but it also means that the freedom they allow themselves is not worthy of the name. Sartre and I have been more ambitious; it has been our wish to experience 'contingent loves'; but there is one question we have deliberately avoided: how would the third person feel about our arrangement? It often happened that the third person accommodated himself to it without difficulty; our union left plenty of room for loving friendships and fleeting affairs. But if the protagonist wanted more, then conflicts would break out ... Although my understanding with Sartre has lasted for more than thirty years, it has not done so without some losses and upsets in which the 'others' always suffered.

Nowhere here is there a sign of the lived torment that Simone herself suffered. The token mention of the pain caused to others smacks again of Beauvoir's need to rationalize away any distress, her evasiveness when she is threatened by a complexity of emotions which she cannot altogether control. It is also, plainly, insensitive. Algren's accusation of passionlessness is certainly justified, as, in part, is the image he evokes of Beauvoir as a spinsterish schoolteacher telling everyone to pull up their moral socks.

No chronicler of our lives since Theodore Dreiser had combined so steadfast a passion for human justice with a dullness so asphyxiating as Mme de Beauvoir. While other writers reproach the reader gently, she flattens his nose against the blackboard, gooses him with a twelve-inch ruler, and warns him if he doesn't start acting grown-up she's going to hold her breath till he does.

Algren's pithiness is fused by passion. He is worth quoting at length.

No other modern writer has moved millions of women, leading submerged lives, towards lives of their own while leading her own vicariously. No other writer has exposed the myths of femininity so lucidly while guarding her own so jealously. Her humanitarianism would be irrefutable if it weren't for men and women getting in the way.

But it is when Algren turns to the whole matter of contingent loves, that he is at his fiercest:

Anybody who can experience love contingently has a mind that has recently snapped. How can love be *contingent?* Contingent upon *what?* The woman is speaking as if the capacity to sustain Man's basic relationship – the physical love of woman and man – were a mutilation; while freedom consists of 'maintaining through all deviations a certain fidelity'! What she means, of course, when stripped of its philosophical jargon, is that she and Sartre erected a facade of *petit-bourgeois* respectability behind which she could continue the search for her own femininity. What Sartre had in mind when *he* left town, I'm sure I don't know.

Procurers are more honest than philosophers. They name this *How-about-a-quickie-kid* gambit as 'chippying' and regard the middle-class woman who indulges herself in it with less respect than they give the fireship who shoves a shiv into a faithless lover's anatomy. The true mutilation, to them, is not passion, but passionlessness; and loving too violently is a lesser affliction than being able to love only contingently. Because it means she is able to live only contingently.

Obviously Algren's male vanity had suffered a shattering blow. Obviously, too, he spoke from within a particularly American ethic which has it that experience, and above all passionate experience, is the measure of all things. Simone's loyalty and attraction to the intellectual Sartre, her own desire to control experience rather than submerge herself in it, was incomprehensible to him.

Nonetheless, the tawdriest side of Beauvoir's and Sartre's lives lies in their treatment of their contingent lovers, 'others'

111

whose individual freedom they severely constricted and in some cases oppressed. They *used* others, but perhaps no more than Simone herself was used by Sartre. With Algren she had greedily attempted to have her cake and eat it – engage in a passionate love and maintain her intellectual and comradely marriage with Sartre. Had she been the man to Algren's woman, there is little question that he, like Dolores, might have been willing to move to France and carry on writing from there. But the woman Simone could not submerge her life in his and live in America. Neither could she easily give him up. She was a woman divided against herself. In *The Mandarins*, the end of Anne's affair leads her to the verge of suicide. Simone herself fell ill and underwent an operation which she was relieved to learn did not reveal the need for a mastectomy. The internal contradictions of leading an independent woman's life are many and far greater than Simone de Beauvoir was willing to acknowledge in her own autobiography.

SIX

The Committed Intellectual

From the time of the publication of *The Second Sex* in 1949 Simone de Beauvoir began increasingly to lead the public life of a writer and left-wing intellectual committed to political and social change. In France this means somewhat more than it does in the Anglo-American world. It is impossible to imagine Ronald Reagan quoting a contemporary philosopher. But it was quite possible for President de Gaulle to take into account Jean-Paul Sartre's position on a given matter and quip that he would allow him to be President of the Left Bank of Paris. The sheer volume of sales of Simone de Beauvoir's books, her presence in a popular press which assiduously tracked her movements and pronouncements is comparable to that of a film or pop star. When Sartre died in 1980 hundreds of thousands of people followed his funeral cortège through the streets of Paris. The French newspaper, *Libération*, on the occasion of Beauvoir's death in 1986, devoted its entire front page to a photograph of her simply headlined, UNE FEMME – a woman. The next twelve pages chronicled and commented on her achievement. It is in the light of this that Sartre's and Beauvoir's activities and

political and intellectual confrontations from the fifties onwards need to be viewed. They became the intellectual ambassadors of the left, travelling to international peace conferences and tribunals, bringing news to Europe of conditions
in distant parts of the globe, lending their names to important liberation struggles or radical causes. In these activities,
in the eyes of the world, they constituted a pair. The public
face of their union helps, in part, to explain its im-
permeability to 'contingent' loves. Individual passion
became secondary to public responsibility.

During the late forties and into the mid fifties two related
issues dominated French intellectual politics. How could
another configuration, greater in scale than that of World
War II best be avoided and peace maintained in a world
which had just witnessed the horror of Hiroshima? Did humanity's best hope lie in socialism – distinct from or akin to
the communism of the Soviet bloc – or capitalism and the
American way of life? Increasingly it began to be apparent
that neither of these questions could be construed without
taking into account the Third World of emerging nations
and liberation struggles. Sartre, Beauvoir and the editorial
group of *Les Temps Modernes* played an active part in under-
lining the importance of this last point to Europeans.

It is easily forgotten that the post-war euphoria over the
defeat of fascism was almost instantly followed by the panic
that another war was imminent. By 1947, the Soviet Union
and the United States were no longer allies and had drawn
up their Cold War positions, with the United States assuming
that Western Europe, beneficiary of the Marshall Plan,

would follow the American line without questions. France's colonial war in Vietnam and the Korean war followed each other in close succession. The Soviet repression of the Hungarian uprising and the Suez crisis came only a few years later in 1956. In France, the brief flowering of socialist hope, inspired by the heroism of the Communist-led Resistance, soon gave way to divisions among the left and to a cold-war enshrinement of the right. Sartre and Beauvoir initially urged people to reject a cold-war politics which divided the world into two opposed blocs. As socialists, their relationship with the USSR was yet a critical one: 'For us, the USSR was the country which embodied socialism, but also one of the two Great Powers hatching a new war ... and thereby putting the world in danger.'

In 1948, Sartre became the virtual leader of the Rassemblement Démocratique Révolutionnaire (RDR) which urged the population not to fall into the trap of cold warriorism and take sides between East and West. Instead, by forging links with other Europe groupings, it sought to construct a European independent of the two blocs and in the forefront of peace. Sartre hoped that the RDR could find support among middle-class reformists as well as the communist working class.

But by 1949 the Red scare was on; communism and socialism were under attack in France. Sartre recognized that the RDR was ineffectual in terms of practical politics and that non-alliance or neutrality were virtually impossible. He and Beauvoir identified with the socialist movement as a whole. As he explained, it 'is the absolute judge of all other movements because the exploited experience exploitation

SIMONE DE BEAUVOIR

and the class struggle as their reality and as the fundamental truth of bourgeois societies ... Socialism is the absolute standard of reference by which any political undertaking is to be judged.'

Refusing to fall prey to the hysteria of anti-communism, highly critical of American politics, particularly in respect to the Third World, and the hate-mongering of the US propaganda machine, Beauvoir and Sartre could not however deny the existence of Soviet labour camps. *Les Temps Modernes* printed one of the first European exposés of Stalin's gulag. The duty of the intellectual was first and foremost to tell the truth, whatever his or her political inclination. Yet as adamant as they were in their criticism of the Soviet Union, Sartre and Beauvoir refused to wipe the Russian experiment out of socialist history and pretend that it had nothing to do with the development of a socialist reality. This uncompromising position made them prey to attacks from all sides: the Gaullist right, the liberal left, for refusing to dispense with the Soviet Union outright, and from the Communists for criticizing the Soviet Union at all. Beauvoir was refused a visa to the US, because of the position of *Les Temps Modernes*, even though she never belonged to any party.

During these cold-war years, Beauvoir's and Sartre's refusal to denounce communism outright and their criticism of McCarthyite America lost them many old friends – amongst them the philosopher Raymond Aron and Albert Camus. Though the break with Camus finally came over a highly critical review of his book, *The Rebel*, in *Les Temps Modernes*, political differences had already served to estrange the friends. Whereas Camus's position, after his left sympathies during the Occupation, had now become a liberal one, Sartre and Beauvoir had moved to the left. Increasingly, particularly for Sartre, it was the oppressed of the world who needed to be given a voice. The United States, because of its imperialism, posed a far greater threat to global peace than the USSR.

Less directly active in politics than Sartre, still shy of committees and platforms, Simone, in these years, put her energies into her work with *Les Temps Modernes* and what was to be her most important novel, *The Mandarins*. The book is an inspired re-creation of French intellectual life and the political forces which shaped it in the period following the euphoria of Liberation. All the hatreds, the intrigues, the hopes and disillusionments experienced in a nation which had been internally divided during the war and where survival went hand in hand with the guilt and bitter memory of friends lost are evoked with the assurance of a writer who is at ease with her craft. Beauvoir had considered calling the book *The Survivors* and the fact of survival informs everything in this world, from the political divisions between the characters to their inner conflicts, from their greed for life to their suicidal despair.

In *Force of Circumstance*, Beauvoir describes how she set out to

reveal the multiple and intricately spun meanings of that changed world to which I awoke in August 1944 ... The practical side of politics – committees, meetings, manifestoes, discussions – bored me as they had always done; but I was interested in all the things that made our world. I had felt what was then called 'the failure of the Resistance' as a personal defeat: the truimphant return of bourgeois domination. My private existence had been deeply affected by it. In stormy quarrels, or else in silence, the friendships that had glowed around me after the Occupation had all more or less died down; their death had become inseparable from the death of the hopes we shared, and that death was the centre around which I organized my book.

Beauvoir's ambitious project of weaving a novel around political and intellectual life in the early years of the Cold War has few equivalents in English-language fiction, probably because of the marginality of intellectuals. Perhaps only Doris Lessing's splendid *The Four-Gated City* evokes a comparably grim post-war London and the malign effects of a world divided between two opposing blocs.

The Mandarins, which like much of Beauvoir's work has an autobiographical core, revolves around two central characters and their various interwoven political and personal lives. Anne is a psychoanalyst married to a writer twenty years her senior, Robert Debreuilh, whose political activity forms the pivotal commitment in his life during the time of the narrative. Like Simone, her heroine is devoted to her husband and his work and she stands in awe of his intellectual trenchancy and political courage. Interestingly, Beauvoir makes Debreuilh into the father figure she always denied Sartre was for her. Interestingly too, her own scepticism about psychoanalysis is at once negated by Anne's and Robert's belief in it ('the possiblilty of rethinking classical psychoanalysis in terms of Marxist ideology struck him as a fascinating idea') and expressed in Anne's disillusionment with her work. Anne and Robert have a daughter, Nadine, who has lost her lover during the war and encapsulates all the bitterness and confusion of post-war youth.

By her own admission, Beauvoir split herself into two characters in the book, putting those things which were directly linked to her condition as a woman into Anne, while her professional anxieties and optimism, 'her pen' were incorporated into the male character, Henri.

I lent her [Anne] tastes, feelings, reactions and memories that were mine; often I speak through her mouth. Yet she has neither my appetites, nor my insistences, nor above all, has she the autonomy that has been bestowed on me by a profession which means so much to me . . . Because she does not have aims and projects of her own, she lives, the 'relative' life of a 'secondary' being. It was mainly the negative aspects of my experience that I expressed through her: the fear of dying and the panic of nothingness, the vanity of earthly diversions, the shame of forgetting, the scandal of living. The joy of existence, the gaiety of activity, the pleasure of writing, all those I bestowed on Henri.

Henri is a writer and journalist, like Camus – with whom many have identified him, though Beauvoir denies this – the editor of a Resistance newspaper which is attempting to retain its independence and readership within the changing political affiliations of the post-war world. Beauvoir's intention was that both Anne and Henri should define themselves in relationship to the Debreuilh-Sartre character, portrayed only through their eyes, with the effect that Debreuilh, like Pierre in *She Came to Stay*, is once again beyond criticism, despite the fact that he is hardly an ideal father or husband.

Through her two central characters Beauvoir narrates the hopes and failures of the RDR, the savagery of war-time and then cold-war politics which divided families and friends. Death stalks the book. At the beginning of the narrative, Anne is in a state of despair: '. . . with the horrifying past behind us, how can anyone have faith in the future? Diego [her daughter's lover] is dead, too many others have died; shame has returned to the earth, the word "happiness" has lost all meaning. All around me nothing but chaos again. Maybe the world *will* pull out of it. But when? Two or three centuries are much too long.'

Though *The Mandarins* is a powerful chronicle of its historical and political moment, at the core of its dramatic action are two separate love stories, mirroring one another. Anne and Debreuilh, for all their mutual loyalty and friendship, no longer share a bed: 'It's been years since we lost our desire for each other, but we were too closely bound in other ways to attach any great importance to the union of our bodies. Therefore we had, so to speak, lost nothing.' Again, as in her earlier fiction, Beauvoir exonerates the Sartre character; yet Anne experiences a living death, watches her body ageing with an anguished stoicism, until during a trip to an American psychoanalytic congress, she meets Lewis Brogan, who is by Beauvoir's own admission a portrait of Nelson Algren, to whom the book is dedicated. With Brogan, Anne comes alive, is transformed into a totally new woman. 'He knew neither my country, my language, my friends nor my worries, only my voice, my eyes, my skin. But I had no other reality than that skin, that voice, those eyes.'

Beauvoir's portrayal of this relationship and its break up, however powerful, nowhere strays from the traditional romantic image of a woman transformed, submerged and eventually broken by love. She has been attacked from feminist quarters for not presenting a 'positive' heroine in Anne, 'a woman who assumed an equal role with men in the realm of professional and political responsibility'. Her justification is that she depicted women as she knew them: divided. Even given this, it is still surprising that with her keen insight into mystifications, Beauvoir neither questions the nature of romantic passion nor the convention that women are the caretakers of emotional experience in the novel's history as a whole.

What she does do is give Anne a modicum of freedom by ensuring that she accepts responsibility for her own life and returns to her work – though 'she does not succeed in finding fulfilment in her undertakings'. And she provides a foil for Anne's experience and ultimate choice of returning to France and her husband in Paule, Henri's mistress, who is her most anguished depiction of a 'woman in love' – in the terms of *The Second Sex*, 'a woman radically alienated from herself by an exclusive attachment to one man, and tyrannizing him in the name of her own slavery'. The juxtaposition of this love affair with Anne's suggests that if Anne's choice had been otherwise, if Anne's choice had led her to accept Brogan/Algren's proposal, she too would have been totally submerged and destroyed by love. Paule's all-consuming jealousy, her clinging to traditional female values, effectively chases Henri away, and leads her to madness.

In 1954 *The Mandarins* was awarded the coveted French literary award, the Prix Goncourt. Simone, after the ferocious attacks on *The Second Sex*, was surprised by its enthusiastic reception from both left- and right-wing critics. Only the Catholic faction still saw in her work, the incarnation of sin: *The Mandarins*, like *The Second Sex*, was placed on the Papal list of forbidden literature for its purported celebration of free love and its attack on the sanctity of the family.

With the Goncourt prize money, Simone finally bought her own flat, a studio overlooking the Montparnasse Cemetery. Her joy in furnishing it, in arranging her prize possessions – her Picasso, her lapidary, a gift from Giacometti, souvenirs of her numerous travels – was great. When she moved into the flat, she thought that this would be the workroom in which she would end her days, the bed she would die in – and indeed, Simone, after her restless itinerary from one hotel room to another, did not move again.

She was forty-six when she was awarded the Prix Goncourt. The affair with Algren had ended three years earlier, bringing in its train a deep depression and a sudden realization of age. Like Anne in *The Mandarins*, Simone felt herself sinking into death at the thought that 'she would never sleep again warmed by another body':

The void had always frightened me, but till now I had been dying day by day without paying attention to it; suddenly at one blow, a whole piece of myself was being engulfed before my eyes . . . In the glass my face still looked the same; behind me a burning past was still not far away, but, in the long years stretching ahead of me, it would not flame up again . . . I suddenly found myself at the other side of a line, though there was no one moment when I had crossed it.

Her cancer scare followed shortly afterwards and then the miracle of finding herself whole. Convalescence was a joyous time and 'when the opportunity arose of coming back to life, I seized it gladly'.

Several new additions had been made to the editorial board of *Les Temps Modernes*. Among them was a young man in his mid twenties, forthrightly and proudly Jewish, who had founded a resistance organization while still at secondary school and had fought in the *maquis*: Claude Lanzmann. Bursting with energy, ideologically in agreement with the Communists, though not a party member, his optimism while sometimes irritating Simone, yet provided a foil to her own pessimism – 'he needed a vision of a redeemed future to compensate for the laceration he suffered'. Lanzmann's spontaneity, his lack of restraint, his excesses of joy and revulsion at once reminded Simone of her own youthful frenzies and provided a counterpart to her and Sartre's emotional puritanism. At the age of forty-four, Simone embarked on a relationship with a man seventeen years her junior and for the first time engaged on the project of living with another person.

In Josée Dayan's film portrait of Simone de Beauvoir, Simone asks Lanzmann what impression she first made on him:

Lanzmann: I found you very beautiful, you had a smooth face and I wanted to see what lay behind your impassivity.

Simone: And then you found that I was less impassive than I looked.

Lanzmann: Oh absolutely. I could give evidence of it, but I don't know if I ought to talk about that . . . What was striking about you right from the beginning, was your taste for life, your constant projects. You always wanted to do something, to travel, to see things in detail . . . It was most surprising to discover the world with you, which was in effect what I did.

With Lanzmann, Simone came back to life. His presence freed her from her age, relieved her of the anxiety attacks she had begun to suffer from with increasing acuteness, and renewed her interest in everything: 'After two years in which the universal marasma had coincided for me with the break up of a love affair and the first warning of decline, I leapt back enthralled into happiness.' They lived together and travelled together with the maniacal intensity which Simone put into the process. It was Lanzmann who encouraged her to carry on working on *The Mandarins*, when Sartre – still Beauvoir's first and foremost critic – was dissatisfied with it, he who gave her the book's title.

In fact, Simone had been afraid that her new partnership with Lanzmann would affect her relationship with Sartre. But it continued as before, though the emphasis now was on the closeness of old and intimate friends and workmates. There is a sense in which Sartre had always used Simone's 'necessary' presence as a protection from over-involvement with other women and this he could easily continue to do, whether she was living with Lanzmann or not. Though his affair with Dolores was now over, he was involved with a variety of women, including Michelle Vian and, soon, the young Evelyne Rey, Lanzmann's actress sister. He had moved into his mother's flat and there Simone worked with him every afternoon. The bouts of high blood pressure, exhaustion and illness – effectively induced by the ferocity with which he drove himself and compounded by too much alcohol and too many drugs – had already begun. Though he refused to acknowledge them, they were to plague him from then onwards for the rest of his life. Simone, whose obsession with death was the reverse coin of her ceaseless activity, began to worry and increasingly to take on the role of Sartre's guardian and nurse, trying to limit his consumption of intoxicants and prevent him from exhausting himself. Every summer until Sartre's death, the two of them took a break from their other relationships to spend two to three months in Rome, which they loved because of the warmth and openness of the left intellectuals who were their friends, and because of the atmosphere of the city as a whole.

In 1955 Sartre and Beauvoir together took part in the Helsinki Peace Conference where representatives from all corners of the world were gathered, including a host of notable writers and intellectuals from both East and West. The Cold War was thawing. Stalin was dead and the Soviet Union seemed to be embarking on a more liberal policy. Sartre's relationship with the Communist Party in France was now a good one and the nation as a whole was looking towards friendly relations with the Soviet Union. Beauvoir notes that 'for us, the Iron Curtain had dissolved; no further embargo, no more exile; the realms of socialism were now part of our world'. Conciliation was the order of the day and it was ironically the Russian writer, Ilya Ehrenburg, who asked Sartre not to attack the USA too fiercely in his contribution to the conference proceedings. Simone, who had spent the preceding years immersed in *The Mandarins* and in her private affairs, felt old urges begin to awaken in her. She wanted to be useful in some way. The Algerian delegation at the conference called for a meeting with the French and informed them that the Algerian rebellion against French colonial rule had entered a new phase. It would be best if the French left the country without a full scale war of independence breaking out. Already reports were filtering through of tortures carried out by the French police. Soon after Beauvoir returned to Paris, a state of emergency was announced in Algeria and a committee was formed which pledged itself to keep Algeria French at any cost. Simone's work on behalf of the Algerian struggle for liberation from France was to form her primary political commitment over the next years. But first there was her confrontation with China.

In the autumn of 1955 Beauvoir and Sartre were invited to China by the Chinese government so that they could report back to the West on the progress of the revolution. The trip was to provide the basis for her book on China, *The Long March*, and for her nascent consciousness of the real meaning of under-development. Her eurocentricity was now tempered by a sense that the mass of the world's population lived lives which bore no relation to hers. The very meaning of words such as field, peasant, village, town, family took on a radically new sense and upset her old touchstones.

Until then, despite my wide reading and my few perfunctory glimpses of Mexico and Africa, I had taken the prosperity of Europe and the United States as my norm, and the rest of the world had existed only vaguely, somewhere on the horizon. Seeing the masses of China upset my whole idea of our planet; from then on it was the Far East, India, Africa, with their chronic shortage of food, that became the truth of the world, and our Western comfort merely a limited privilege.

It should be noted that this perception of Beauvoir's, although hardly unusual now, came at a time when most European intellectuals were still solidly entrenched in a world composed only of Eastern and Western blocs.

On her return to Paris, Simone engaged in lengthy research before writing her essay which attempts to examine the Chinese revolution in the light of its own history, rather than through the eyes of a Western critic. Already in that year her essay on 'Right-wing Thought Today' ('La pensée de droite aujourd'hui') had attacked the bourgeoisie for attempting to universalize a moribund system of ideas. Now she sought to rid herself of her own European blinkers. Westerners in the fifties were rarely given the opportunity to visit China and see the revolution at work for themselves. Beauvoir was eager to counteract the flood of anti-revolutionary propaganda issuing from Hong Kong. Thus her book stresses the positive aspects of the revolution, the fact that Chinese adaptations of communism have an altogether practical component and, most importantly, that China is the only large under-developed nation to have won the battle against hunger. In their construction of socialism, the Chinese people had overcome the traditional scourges of pre-revolutionary China – dirt, vermin, epidemics, infant mortality, chronic malnutrition. Because women, too, were needed in the work of reconstruction, their status became a far more equitable one than had ever been the case before. It was, in Beauvoir's assessment, a laudable beginning. China restored her confidence in history.

French government policy in Algeria, however, shook it severely. Beauvoir recognized that eventually Algeria would have to emerge as an independent nation – but at what cost? From 1956, when reports of French torture of Algerians began to circulate in France, until 1962 when independence was finally won, Beauvoir and Sartre waged one of their most sustained campaigns on behalf of liberation. They wrote, they broadcast, they spoke on public platforms and they demonstrated. Their activities initially earned them attacks of treachery, accusations of demoralizing the nation and of treason.

At the time of the escalation of the war in Algeria, France – including at first the left which feared it would lose popular support – was determinedly behind a government which had come to the aid of the French colonists in Algeria, the *Pieds Noirs*, against the growing insurgency of the native Muslim population. 'Giving not a thought to what it was going to cost, convinced that "the loss of Algeria" would make them poorer, their mouths full of slogans and clichés – French Empire, French departments, abandonment, selling out, grandeur, honour, dignity – the entire population of the country . . . were caught up in a great tide of chauvinism and racism,' Beauvoir writes in *Force of Circumstance*. Torture, rape, no tactics were too brutal for the French army, while the FLN (Front de Libération Nationale) were accused of 'Islamic barbarity' for their guerrilla attacks. Increasingly Simone began to feel like an exile in her own country. Even the Communists in 1956 were no longer potential allies: she and Sartre had signed a protest against the Soviet invasion of Hungary categorically condemning Soviet aggression and Sartre had broken off relations with his friends in the Soviet Union. They had broken even more definitively with those responsible for the policies of the French Communist Party whose propaganda organs perpetrated lies about the nature of the Hungarian uprising.

The Algerian crisis escalated and the colonial struggle found its resonance within France itself. Algerians within

France were the daily victims of man-hunts, while the French turned a blind eye. When the *Dossier Müller* – a French soldier's report on the atrocities committed in Algeria which testified that entire battalions were looting, burning, raping and massacring, and that torture had become a normal method for extracting information – arrived at *Les Temps Modernes*, Simone, usually far more sanguine about political events than Sartre, was revolted and impassioned. She could no longer bear her fellow citizens and rarely went out: 'I felt as dispossessed as I had when the occupation began.' *Les Temps Modernes* called for the independence of the Algerian people and bravely asserted its sympathy for the tactics of the FLN.

In 1958, unsettled by the Algerian war, plagued by internal divisions, an increasing number of strikes and civil unrest, France underwent a major governmental crisis. Only de Gaulle, who had the support of the army, could, it was thought, save the day and reinstate law and order. No one knew what his policy on Algeria would in fact be, but it was assumed that it would be a nationalistic one. Beauvoir and Sartre campaigned and demonstrated against his return and against the 1958 referendum which radically altered the constitution so as to give the president greater powers. Beauvoir's spirits fell even further as she recognized that bourgeois democracy preferred to accept a dictator than to revive a popular front government. France's entire political future seemed to be at stake. For her and for Sartre, the new constitution marked an enormous collective suicide. As Sartre put it in his letter from Brazil to the military court which was trying a friend and co-worker for his activities on behalf of the FLN:

The independence of [Algeria] ... is a certain fact. What is not certain is the future of democracy in France. For the war in Algeria has made this country rotten. The increasing restriction of liberties, the disappearance of political life, the general acceptance of the use of torture, the permanent opposition of the military to the civil power, are all marks of a development which one can without exaggeration qualify as Fascist.

The immediate effect of Sartre's statement was a call in the French Assembly for legal action to be taken against him.

Beauvoir's direct action at this time included a fierce campaign for the reprieve of a death sentence against a former student of hers who had been involved in a bombing attempt in Algeria. In 1960, she engaged her efforts on behalf of Djamila Boupacha, a young Algerian woman tortured by the French who was prepared to take the French army to court. Her lawyer wanted the trial to take place in France. Beauvoir wrote an article for the newspaper *Le Monde* which was banned that day in Algiers, though because of her intervention, the case took on international moment. Simone became part of the Djamila Boupacha defence committee and wrote a preface to the book about her.

Again in 1960 *Les Temps Modernes* published the 'Manifesto of the 121' which stated that individuals could justifiably dodge the draft in the case of the Algerian war. This constituted an incitement to civil disobedience and a risk of five years in prison. In Brazil, where Sartre and Beauvoir were travelling, there were rumours of Sartre's imminent arrest on his return to Paris. Five thousand veterans of the war marched down the Champs Elysées shouting 'Shoot Sartre'. Beauvoir and Sartre would have liked to give as much publicity to the cause of the draft resisters as possible by having themselves arrested, but although charges were made, the trial was postponed and soon charges were withdrawn. De Gaulle was too astute a politician to allow himself to be seen arresting an intellectual with an international reputation. As he remarked, 'One doesn't arrest Voltaire.'

Growing popular support for the liberation of Algeria led to the birth of the terrorist OAS, which launched its bomb attacks throughout France as a reprisal against the anticolonialists. Sartre's residences – and he and Beauvoir moved several times during this period to keep one step ahead of the terrorists – were bombed several times in 1961–2. When Beauvoir's co-authored book on Djamila Boupacha appeared, a phone call threatening assassination was made to her flat.

The prolonged struggle for Algerian independence marked Beauvoir definitively as an engaged intellectual whose writing was a form of political activity, primary amongst others. During these years of political passion, there was no possibility of turning away from public responsibility. Yet it was also during these years that Simone began to look back on her own life and dissect the forces that had shaped her. Paradoxically, her autobiography became one of her greatest public statements: 'I am an intellectual. I take words and truth to be of value,' she writes in *Force of Circumstance*, describing her revulsion at the miasma of lies which pervaded France during the early days of the Algerian war. In her autobiography, it is the truth she looks for within her own past, so as to make this, too, 'public' and blur the divisions which separate the political from the personal.

SEVEN

The Exemplary Life

Simone de Beauvoir began to write her autobiography at the age of forty-eight. *Memoirs of a Dutiful Daughter* appeared two years later. The most sustained and 'finished' narrative of the four-volume sequence, it recounts Simone's Catholic childhood, adolescence, rebellion and young womanhood until her meeting with Sartre and the death of Zaza. It was followed in 1960 by *The Prime of Life*, the record of her early life with Sartre, her literary apprenticeship, her first published novel and the harrowing years of the Second World War which gave birth to existentialism and her and Sartre's ethics of commitment. *Force of Circumstance* appeared in 1963 and records the period of cold-war politics, the Algerian struggle, and the years of political activism. Then there was a long gap until 1972, when the final volume, *All Said and Done*, appeared. Here Beauvoir gave up her loosely chronological structure and recapitulated the entirety of her life, only then focusing on the thematic clusters which preoccupied her and formed the fabric of her life in later years. Her overall purpose in writing this monumental autobiography, which must count amongst her foremost achievements, was 'to make myself exist for others by conveying, as directly as I could, the taste of my own life'. Together, these four weighty volumes, replete with historical, cultural and personal detail, construct a life which is as important a project as *The Second Sex* or any of Beauvoir's fiction.

Autobiography is traditionally the prerogative of the person of action, rather than the person of letters, and of the man at that, rather than the woman. Beauvoir's memoirs are thus unique on two counts. They set out to isolate and identify her 'own particular brand of femininity' and serve as a record of a life lived in part in the public eye. The autobiographer's work of unveiling is always simultaneously a labour of imaginative reconstruction in which the many faces and moments of the self take on the unity, even if discontinuous, of a narrative. Past becomes here an inevitable apprenticeship to the present. Present interests signal and underline past meanings as well as occasionally evading them. Beauvoir, with all her emphasis on 'the truth and sincerity' of her undertaking can be no exception to this. She herself is aware that the work of memory is a work of creation which endows experience with 'artistic necessity'.

Beauvoir's autobiography creates a model life for that heroine which is herself. The figure who emerges from the memoirs is a woman who has fulfilled her childhood ambition to know and write as honestly as possible, a woman who has sucessfully asserted her liberty, transcended woman's condition of otherness to become a subject, and engaged in the responsible, committed life of a post-war intellectual. There is a sense that rough edges have been smoothed over, that internal contradictions have not been altogether fully confronted. Sexuality, anxieties, bouts of deep depression, are all treated evasively, as indeed is the whole question of Simone's own femininity.

I suspect that side-by-side with genuine admiration, the irritation sometimes generated by the autobiography and its calm authority rests on two related features of the work. One is that Beauvoir criticizes herself just enough to undermine any further criticism. She is quick to assess and attack her own illusions. The optimism of *The Prime of Life* is shown to be based on a false notion of freedom underpinned by bourgeois privilege; her own belief in the indomitability of her will is tempered by war and circumstance. Beauvoir truthfully calls attention to her own blindnesses and jealousies, only to pass over them quickly and leave them effectively unexplored. Nowhere is this clearer than in her 'identification' of her own femininity which she claims was never at issue: 'I did not deny my femininity any more than I took it for granted. I simply ignored it.'

In many ways the autobiography continues to ignore it, perhaps precisely because of the second factor: Beauvoir's age. At the time that she begins the autobiography and particularly by the time she arrives at the sections which constitute the middle two volumes, she is already an older woman whose thoughts are focused less on sexuality, relationships with men and on her own femininity than on ageing, illness, death. Those excesses and uncertainties we expect from youth are veiled over by a habit of reason and reasonableness which is now Beauvoir's daily home. Extremes of early individual passion seem a bit of an embarrassment and are treated in a cursory way. There is only rarely a hint of female masochism. The host of difficulties which characterized her early years with Sartre, her loves, her developing sense of herself as a woman all belong to a past which has been transcended. This, combined with the value Beauvoir places on the rational, results in what is sometimes an irritating discrepancey between the experience she charts and the coolly reasonable tone in which she does so – a tone which judiciously avoids the heights and depths of emotional drama. Interestingly, it is when she presents us with chunks from her diaries of an earlier period – as she does for part of the war years – that the autobiography springs into a different, more emotive key; or when she recounts recent political battles such as the Algerian war; or evokes the impact of ageing when the sense of a future recedes from the world.

What Beauvoir gives us in the autobiography is precisely what some have criticized her for not giving Anne in *The Mandarins* – a full life which does not centre only on the traditional domains of women's experience, the emotions and sexuality. Instead, work, projects, the public, historical and cultural spheres are placed side by side with this experience. On balance, the public sphere holds greater weight. Our perception of this is exacerbated by the fact that recent years have brought us ample numbers of women's confessionals each probing in detail the specificty of women's emotional and sexual lives, so that the relative absence of this in the memoirs of a woman who paved the way for such explorations forcibly strikes the contemporary eye. But Beauvoir's roots lie in a reticent and more puritanical generation. There is a double absurdity here: the first lies in asking Beauvoir to compose the memoirs of a woman brought up in a different epoch and reared on an assimilation of *The Second Sex*; the second in feeling irritated with her for not delving deeply enough into those very areas which women have increasingly rejected as containing the *totality* of their possible experience.

This said, it is also clear that Beauvoir partly set out to write her memoirs in order to counter the attacks made on her by critics when *The Second Sex* appeared. In a 1960 interview she states that she wanted to correct a prevalent misunderstanding about her: that *The Second Sex* was written at the age of forty out of a sense of feminine rancour by a woman who wanted to revenge herself for a life which had been totally miserable and had made her bitter. The full and exemplary life she evokes in the memoirs certainly puts paid to any notion of an embittered female trapped in her own condition.

Beauvoir's particular aim of answering the critics also helps to explain – without explaining away – the various passages in the memoirs where she is concerned to emphasize that she never suffered on account of her femininity and was always accepted as an 'equal without difference' by her circle of friends.

It is also true that the Beauvoir who emerges from the memoirs is a women adept at suppression – a suppression which allows her to get on with the business of life and achievement. Never altogether sympathetic to a psychoanalytic approach which might endanger her sense of self-control, her hold on a lucid consciousness, she admits that the 'truth' of the memoirs is the particular 'truth of her own universe'.

... My love of truth far exceeds my concern for my own image: that love is explained by my own history, and I take no credit for it. In short because I offer no judgment of myself, I feel no resistance to speaking frankly about my own life and myself, at least in so far as I place myself within my own universe. Perhaps my image projected in a different world – that of the psychoanalysts – might disconcert or embarrass me. But so long as it is I who paint my own portrait, nothing daunts me.

The portrait that emerges in the autobiography is indeed a daunting one. Like the most enterprising of Balzacian heroes, Simone de Beauvoir overcomes the constraints of class and gender, to earn a place in the world – first as a brilliant student, then as a teacher, a woman who earns her own independent living, then as the lover and companion of the most reputed philosopher of his age, finally as an acclaimed writer and leading figure of the left and of the feminist movement. Throughout her long life there is evidence of that intellectual liveliness and clarity which sweeps away 'cant and humbug' in a vast enterprise of demystification. In the midst of all this, time is used with a devouring energy, to read history, fiction, philosphy; to go to innumerable films and plays; to travel with the voracious curiosity, sense of adventure and attention to detail of an eighteenth-century figure engaged on a grand tour of the world; to engage in friendships and love affairs, as well as manage and maintain harmony amongst the not inconsequential number of liaisons that Sartre amassed and kept.

Inevitably there are suppressions, evasions, choices of 'particular' truths and omission of others. As Angela Carter has mischievously, and altogether accurately, pointed out: 'One of the most interesting projects of the life of Simone de Beauvoir has been her mythologization of Sartre. Her volumes of memoirs are devoted to this project.' Indeed the Sartre of the memoirs, as absent in person as he is present in greatness, is a formidable figure. Always cleverer than she, always more correct in his philosophical and political positions than any one else, always at hand to help, to discuss work or relations, never angry or resentful and hardly resented for his inveterate Don Juanism, the Sartre here is neither the Sartre of Beauvoir's letters to Algren, nor the Sartre of his recent biographers. In an important way, however, Simone, always the dutiful daughter, needed throughout her life to keep Sartre distant, intractable, and as he appeared in her dreams: 'the stony-hearted man unmoved by my reproaches, tears, prayers or fainting'. The presence of absolute authority, incarnated in 'the greatest philosopher of his time', allowed her at once to keep rebelling and to keep achieving. Sartre's constant presence in the memoirs as one of the terms of the 'we' Beauvoir uses, is also a means of stamping or labelling Sartre as primarily part of the Sartre–Beauvoir duo. It will be impossible for future historians to mistake any of Sartre's other women, the lead actresses in his plays, for example, as his key partner in life. Through the autobiography, Simone indelibly leaves her omnipresent mark on his life.

It was only after Sartre's death that Simone could permit a different image of Sartre to emerge: the often childish and promiscuous Sartre of the *Letters au Castor*, the *Letters to the Beaver*, edited by Simone and published in 1983 after his death, who always tells her how he loves her and then asks her not to reveal the fact of his letter to Olga or Wanda or whoever is the mistress of the moment. Nor, more revealingly in terms of Beauvoir's own feelings, is he the exasperating, sometimes pathetic and petty figure who emerges in her *Adieux*, her tribute to Sartre's last ten years and his death. In its almost brutal frankness of detail about Sartre's illness, his growing blindness and senescence, this moving narrative tells us more about the real quality of their relationship, its strengths and shortfalls, than the many pages of the autobiography. The difficult last years of Sartre's life estranged them politically and strained their friendship. Only after his death could Simone allow herself to show her anger and irritation, as well as the genuine respect and love they shared. It is here that I am finally ready to believe her declaration that the relationship with Sartre was the 'one undoubted success in my life' – though I would judge her achievements somewhat differently. Beauvoir's impact on the women's movement, her role as one of those rare thinkers who has directly affected our way of seeing the world, surely constitutes a greater 'success' than her relationship to Sartre, however we judge his own philosophical and literary legacy.

For all their wealth of detail and honesty, the memoirs are, paradoxically, personal books only in so far as they are public. They are rarely intimate. Simone's life here unfolds in relation to the outside world, through which, as she understands it, the individual defines herself. Beauvoir gives us none of the sense in which the inner, intimate, often secret and unconscious life may shape or fracture the relationship to the external. With her formidable critical capacities, she, herself, suspects this, though she blames it on the formal problem of following a chronological narrative. In the Prologue to *All Said and Done*, she writes:

The reader has the feeling that he is never being given anything but the non-essential, the side-issues – a series of forewords: the heart of the matter always seems to lie somewhere farther on ... every stage of my life was haunted by those I had lived through earlier – my life as an adult by my childhood and adolescence, the war by the years before the war. By following the sequence of time, I put it out of my power to convey these interconnections, this dovetailing; so I failed to give my past hours their threefold dimension: they march by, devoid of life, reduced to the flatness of a never-ending present, cut off from what went before and from what came after.

Yet there was no other way I could have done it. For me life was an undertaking that had a clear direction, and in giving an account of mine I had to follow its progress.

There is only one constellation of feelings in the world of the autobiography which still seems vitally to threaten Beauvoir's clear direction in a way that past affairs, love, and her feminine condition no longer do. These all have to do with death and ageing. Each of the volumes of the autobiography, except the last, end on a note of death – and one senses that this is more than a rhetorical device.

From the time I knew I was mortal I found the idea of death terrifying. Even when the world was at peace and my happiness seemed secure, my fifteen-year-old self would often turn giddy at the thought of that utter non-being – *my* utter non-being that would descend on its appointed day for ever and ever. This annihilation filled me with such horror that I could not conceive the possibility of facing it 'coolly'.

Death haunts Beauvoir in dreams, takes a prominent place in many of her books, is a real presence in her anxiety attacks, and shadows her footsteps which grow quicker as she tries to outdistance it. As an old friend says to her, you've always been too old for your years. With Sartre's illness, a slow degeneration over the last twenty years of his life, her preoccupation with death grows ever greater.

Our death is inside us, but not like the stone in the fruit, like the meaning of our life; inside us, but a stranger to us, an enemy, a thing of fear. Nothing else counts. My books, the criticisms, the letters I get, the people who talk to me about it, everything that would otherwise have given me pleasure, rendered utterly void . . . Death had become an intimate presence to me in 1954, but henceforth it possessed me . . . This subjection had a name: old age.

What Beauvoir fears most is precisely what cannot be incorporated into the project of existence. Her life had always been grounded on a future, for which the present was overcome. The future gone, there is no longer any need for the indomitable will which characterizes her very being. She is a prey to nothingness.

The world around me has changed: it has become smaller and narrower . . . There are no more oddities, madness is no longer 'holy', crowds have lost the power to intoxicate me; youth, which once fascinated me, seems now no more than a prelude to maturity. Reality still interests me, but it no longer reveals itself like an awful lightning flash . . . I have lived stretched out towards the future, and now I am recapitulating, looking back over the past. It's as though the present somehow got left out.

The woman who writes this is fifty-four. She has another twenty-four years to live. It is as if Beauvoir has prepared all her life for this period of age – oddly wanted it. Paradoxically it evokes a seering honesty in her. No longer mutilated, divided by her femininity, she confronts it far more openly in its absence. Admirably, and unlike many of us, she is most honest about what is closest to her rather than about that which is furthest away.

I thought, one day when I was forty: 'Deep in that looking glass, old age is watching and waiting for me; and it's inevitable, one day she'll get me.' She's got me now. I often stop, flabbergasted, at the sight of that incredible thing that serves me as a face. I understand La Castiglione, who had every mirror smashed. I had the impression once of caring very little what sort of figure I cut . . . I loathe my appearance now: the eyebrows slipping down towards the eyes, the bags underneath, the excessive fullness of the cheeks, and that air of sadness around the mouth that wrinkles bring . . .

Yes, the moment has come to say: Never again! . . . Never again a man. Now, not my body alone but my imagination has accepted that. In spite of everything, it's strange not to be a body any more. There are moments when the oddness of it, because it's so definitive, chills my blood. But what hurts more than all these deprivations is never feeling any new desires.

Beauvoir's most moving book comes out of her confrontation with death. *A Very Easy Death* is effectively another chapter in her autobiography and ironically, the most intimate one. In evoking the last days of her mother's life, the humiliation this proud woman suffers at the hands of a medical system dedicated to life at all costs, Beauvoir reassesses a crucial relationship which has been absent from those pages of her autobiography which constructed her adult life.

Here, in the final confrontation between mother and

daughter, buried emotions that she can neither control nor explain away rise up and overwhelm her:

When my father died I did not cry at all. I had said to my sister, 'It will be the same for Maman.' I had understood all my sorrows until that night: even when they flowed over my head I recognized myself in them. This time my despair escaped my control: someone other then myself was weeping in me. I had talked to Sartre about my mother's mouth as I had seen it that morning and about everything I had interpreted in it – greediness refused, an almost servile humility, hope, distress, loneliness – the loneliness of her death and of her life – that did not want to admit its existence. And he told me that my own mouth was not obeying me any more: I had put Maman's mouth on my face and in spite of myself, I copied its movements. Her whole person, her whole being, was concentrated there, and compassion wrung my heart.

For the first time in her adult life, Simone brings into the open an identity with the mother she at once loved and despised. Her entire childhood is before her as well as her own death. The violence of her reaction, the 'hysteria' that all but envelops her in this identification with her mother, suggests that the very aspect of woman's experience she has shunned has now risen to the fore. She is also that woman oppressed by a condition she has always consciously refused. Significantly, it is at this time that Beauvoir's relationship with the young student, Sylvie Le Bon, grows closer. 'The better I knew Sylvie, the more kin I felt to her. She too was an intellectual and she was passionately in love with life. And she was like me in other ways: with thirty-three years of difference, I recognized my qualities and my faults in her.' No longer a daughter, Simone can now accept a symbolic motherhood.

After this moment, there is no real further need for an

autobiography. The impulse is gone. In a psychological sense, as well as on a purely chronological level, Beauvoir has caught up with herself. During the next years, Simone writes two further fictions, each of which are at a distance from herself and explore women trapped by lives not altogether of their own making. The first, *Les Belles Images* (*Beautiful Images*), is an exposé of the hollowness of a technocratic society where ideas and emotions are subsumed in the empty phrases of a publicity copy-writer. A frenzied complacency is the order of the day in this world of the wealthy bourgeoisie. Beauvoir's heroine is 'a young married woman sufficiently in agreement with those around her not to sit in judgment, but also sufficiently honest to feel uneasy about her complicity'. It is her young daughter's persistent questions about children who live in misery which finally punctures her equanimity. Imprisoned, caught in the illusion of the 'good life' from which she can see no escape, her body lives her despair. She falls prey to a violent anorexia by which everyone around her is embarrassed.

In this short, fast-paced, almost brutal narrative, Beauvoir lays bare the fraudulence and emptiness of an affluent society of the sixties which wilfully blinds itself to the fate of the larger part of humanity. Unlike much of her earlier fiction, the only partially autobiographical element in the novel lies in the relationship of the heroine, Laurence, to her father, a pseudo-philosopher whose seemingly attractive morality is based on notions so outworn that they leave him as blind to reality as the other characters of the book. Like Beauvoir, her heroine gradually recognizes the hypocrisy implicit in her admired father's views. But however deeply felt Laurence's condition is, she is not the Simone who has forged the outlines of her own existence.

Beauvoir's next fiction, *The Woman Destroyed*, comprises three separate stories interrelated through their exploration of woman's condition.

I had received the confidences of several women in their forties whose husbands had left them for others: in spite of their differences of character ... the women could not even remotely understand what was happening to them; they thought their husbands' behaviour contradictory, abnormal and deviant, and the rival unworthy of his love: their world was falling to pieces and they ended up by no longer knowing who they were.

Whereas Paule in *The Mandarins* suffers this fate, Beauvoir describes her sufferings from the outside. In *The Woman Destroyed*, the title story of the volume, the portrait of Monique is drawn from within and in diary form. The pathos of a woman whose life has been given over to 'creating happiness' for her husband and family, who has lived vicariously only to find herself stripped of those others who gave her an identity is so acute that it in part obscures Beauvoir's intention of revealing the complicity and self-delusion inherent in such an existence. Monique may weave the very darkness into which she sinks, but our sympathy for her exceeds Beauvoir's conscious grasp on her material, just as Simone's own feelings defied her control in her identification with her mother.

Beauvoir's expressed intent is more evident in the story entitled *The Monologue* because here her anti-heroine is a more extreme case. Using the technique of the inadvertent self-confession, Beauvoir exposes a woman who wilfully

145

blinds herself to the failure of her own life and her responsibility for her daughter's suicide. In order to keep her self-image intact, her heroine twists reality and clothes herself in a paranoid hatred of the external world. Her self-justification only succeeds in damning her in our eyes.

The Age of Discretion, the first story in the volume, evokes the changing nature of an intellectual couple's relations as they enter an old age they experience differently: the woman by refusing it, the man by accepting it too soon. Beauvoir's heroine, here, feels doubly betrayed: by the growing diffidence of her husband and with her son's choice of a career with a government she despises. How can she come to terms with this as well as with the failure of her own most recent work? In this story lies the germ for a larger work which would explore the ramifications of the last phase of life, but Beauvoir never undertook it. *Les Belles Images* and *The Woman Destroyed* were to be her last fictions. Despite their vast sales, criticism was rife. In particular, feminists, feeling betrayed, reproached her for not having created any positive images of contemporary women. There is only one piece of writing in which Beauvoir gives us this and surprisingly it lies in her essay on Brigitte Bardot. Bardot, for Beauvoir, encapsulates that ambiguous nymph, that child-woman who, in an age where the adult woman inhabits the same sphere as man, is still surrounded by the aura of sexual mystery. Yet this mystery is not the traditionally passive one of the erotic female object, but rather an aggressive one. 'She is as much hunter as she is prey. The male is an object to her, just as she is to him,' Beauvoir comments approvingly. BB is a free woman who follows her own inclinations:

She eats when she is hungry and makes love with the same unceremonious simplicity. Desire and pleasure seem to her more convincing than precepts and conventions . . . She does as she pleases, and that is what is disturbing. She does not ask questions, but she brings answers whose frankness may be contagious. Moral lapses can be corrected, but how could BB be cured of that dazzling virtue – genuineness? It is her very substance.

If BB is for Beauvoir the youthful incarnation of the existentialist 'free woman', there is no portrait in her fiction of an equally 'positive' heroine. There is perhaps no need for one. In that monumental work which is her autobiography, Beauvoir had already created her single and most extraordinary exemplary woman: herself.

EIGHT

A Radical Old Age

The last twenty years of Simone de Beauvoir's life were paradoxically her most defiantly radical. Her phenomenal energy remained all but unabated and she threw herself into activity with characteristic recklessness. In her forties, she had learned to drive with some trepidation and much excitement. From then on, the experience of driving – in which memories and expectations merged in a continuous present – never lost its intoxication for her. Neither did travelling or reading. Far more than Sartre and with greater openness, she kept up with the developments which marked French intellectual life in the sixties, when structuralism replaced existentialism as the main theoretical currency. Her lucidity was unimpaired. Simone was prepared to admit where her thinking, particularly in relation to feminism, might have been mistaken in the past. Her criticism of Western capitalism and its dehumanizing effects, of US imperialism and racism, became ever more impassioned. Yet so, too, did her condemnation of the Soviet Union for its attack on human rights, for its violent repression of Czechoslovakia when that country had attempted to throw off the yoke of a police state and introduce a democratic socialism. Despite the increasing political committment of this last phase of her life, her refusal to bow to the dogma and mystifications of any party line or single set of prescriptions about the world was pronounced. What she termed 'cant and humbug' were always her enemies. Her first and foremost responsibility remained to her own intelligence, whatever the moral pressures of any political grouping. Unlike many of us, she grew more radical with age.

Yet these last years of energetic and vociferous radicalism have their underlying melancholy. Old age brought its train of deaths among friends and acquaintances. The management of Sartre's prolonged decline was difficult and painful. Then, too, Simone no longer saw writing as a privileged mode of communication. She felt that many of the young, whom she would particularly have liked to reach, thought reading pointless. This exacerbated the contradiction she and Sartre had already recognized in the early sixties between the intellectual's universal aspirations and the prison of their individual and bounded experience. Her early belief in the value of Western culture, in culture as a whole, was shaken. Nonetheless, she still wished to communicate what in that culture remained valid and might help people to live.

Beauvoir's life had always dove-tailed into her work. Her old age was no exception. Just as the personal experience which had led her to question her femininity had resulted in the writing of *The Second Sex*, so, now, as she moved into her sixties, the experience of growing old fed her mammoth study, *Old Age*. Indeed, *Old Age* is in many respects a book parallel to *The Second Sex*. Certainly the critical reception which greeted its appearance in 1970 was as violent as it had once been for her pioneering study of woman.

The condition of old age, Beauvoir proclaims – as she had earlier done for the condition of women – is a cultural and not merely a biological fact. It, too, has been hidden from history; and its attendant myths enshrine the old in a silent impotence, perhaps even greater than that of women. Drawing on all the analytic tools at her disposal – medical, anthropological, historical, literary and sociological – Beauvoir sets out to break the conspiracy of silence which has made of age a shameful secret. She writes with a vehemence, fuelled by a sense of personal outrage, stripping the veils from a condition we shun but which awaits us all.

Old age, she states, is the human condition in which alienation from oneself is most intense. 'Within me, it is the Other – that is to say the person I am from the outside – who is old: and that Other is myself.' In the eyes of the world, old people read their own abject humiliation. Unproductive, in an epoch which values only productivity, without a future in which their projects could define them, the old are impotent, invisible as individuals separate from the condition of age. Yet this condition has caught them unawares. So absolutely there for everyone to see, age rarely signals its arrival: 'Our private, inward experience, does not tell us the number of our years; no fresh perception comes into being to show us the decline of age.' Trapped in an alien body, excluded from an active place in society, the suffering of the old merely makes the young impatient.

As she did in *The Second Sex*, here Beauvoir probes taboo territory and examines the sexuality of the old. Though the body may decay, she notes, sexual desire often persists. Society, however, refuses to acknowledge this. The old who manifest their desires are seen either as laughing stocks or perverts. For the old woman, this is exacerbated. No space, no iconography exists in our culture for the representation of her desires, through which personal expression or even recognition, could be made possible. To herself and to others the desiring old woman seems mad.

With no future or use, the old suffer the full brunt of redundancy in a society based on production and profit. Beauvoir's denunciation of the capitalist world here reaches its emotive peak.

We are told that retirement is the time of freedom and leisure: poets have sung 'the delights of reaching port'. These are shameless lies. Society inflicts so wretched a standard of living upon the vast majority of old people that it is almost tautological to say 'old and poor' . . . The fact that for the last fifteen or twenty years of his life a man should be no more than a reject, a piece of scrap, reveals the failure of our civilization . . . Those who condemn the maiming, crippling system in which we live should expose this scandal.

Some years after the appearance of *Old Age*, Beauvoir took one more step to 'expose the scandal'. She scripted a film, *La Promenade des Vieux*, which gave visual reality to the condition of the old. Filmed in a state-run old people's home which has all the aspect of a prison, these terrifying images of the old graphically reinforce Beauvoir's statement that 'what is terrifying is not death, but old age and its cortège of injustices'.

To better the general condition of the old, the fundamental values and social structures of the Western world need to be radically altered. On the individual level, Beauvoir writes,

There is only one solution if old age is not to be an absurd parody of our former life, and that is to go on pursuing ends that give our existence meaning – devotion to individuals, to groups or to causes, social, political, intellectual or creative work . . .

Self-avowedly one of the privileged ones, Beauvoir was able in old age to 'go on pursuing those ends which give our existence meaning'. The final phase of her life is exemplary beyond the point of even her own narrative.

Sartre and she continued to travel the globe as intellectual ambassadors who could expose injustice and be counted on to give voice to problems and causes in the presses of the world. In many of the places they visited crowds lined the streets on their arrival and huge numbers of people vied for places at their lectures. Sartre's refusal of the Nobel Prize for Literature in 1964 – because a writer should not allow himself to be turned into an institution and should maintain his independence – had turned him into an even greater celebrity. In 1960 Beauvoir and Sartre visited Brazil, whose left-leaning regime was soon to be victim to a US-aided coup d'état; and Cuba, where they were welcomed by Castro. In 1963 Czechoslovakia and in 1966 Japan and the Soviet Union – where they may have been responsible for obtaining a pardon for the interned poet Joseph Brodsky – welcomed them. The following year they refused an invitation from the Soviet Writers' Union in protest against the condemnation of the writers Sinyavsky and Daniel; and in 1968 they broke with the Soviet Union altogether over the invasion of Czechoslovakia.

When *Les Temps Modernes* was preparing an issue on the Israeli-Arab conflict, Sartre and Simone travelled to the

Middle East where Simone was particularly appalled by the status of women. Amongst other public appearances that Sartre and she made, Simone lectured in Cairo on the position of women and accused Egyptian men of behaving like feudalists, colonialists and racists towards women. Women's inequality, she was told over and over again by the men she met, forms part of the Islamic faith. When President Nasser received their delegation, Simone raised the question of women's inequality with him.

On their return to France, the Seven Days' War broke out and Simone was in a state of extreme anxiety: 'For different reasons I felt a friendship for both countries.' In conflict with many of her younger friends who had not experienced the Nazi extermination of the Jews at first hand during the war, she had strong sympathies for Israel. She did not see how Israel could accurately be defined as a colonialist power. Nor could she see it as a bridgehead for US imperialism, since the US had no military bases there; nor did they draw any wealth from the country – as they did in the Arab states. Yet she wanted Israel to return the occupied territories and 'show itself as determined to make peace as it was to win the war'. Her continued unwillingness to condemn Israel outright brought her the disapproval of the radical left. Although she allied herself with the new left, she would accept neither party line nor moral pressures wholesale.

I regret that the non-Communist left should have grown as monolithic as the Party itself. A left-winger must necessarily admire China without the least reservation, take Nigeria's side against Biafra and the Palestinian's against Israel. I will not bow to these conditions. Yet this does not prevent me from being close to the *gauchistes* in the area in which they are most directly concerned – in the action they carry out in France.

1967 saw the Bertrand Russell Tribunal of War Crimes which placed on trial American action in the Vietnam War. Both Sartre and Beauvoir played a major role in this international 'court of justice'. In its first meeting, the Tribunal sought a response to two questions: had the United States committed an act of aggression as defined by international law; had there been bombing of purely civilian targets and if so to what extent? Reports were read, depositions made and the evidence was far more overwhelming and terrible than Beauvoir had imagined. At the next meeting of the Tribunal, some months later, the scale of atrocities committed by the Americans – as revealed by film footage, the testimony of former US soldiers and Vietnamese victims of torture – was so great that Sartre and Beauvoir were forced to agree, despite their initial hesitation, that there had been acts 'tending towards the extermination of the population and coming within the legal definition of acts of genocide'. Beauvoir's opposition to US policy in her last years grew vehement. In the final summing up of her views which she makes in *All Said and Done*, she writes:

The moment a nationalist or popular movement seems to threaten its interests, the United States crushes it. Millions upon millions of men are kept in a subhuman condition so that the United States may plunder the wealth of the under-developed countries at its ease. What is so scandalously absurd about it all is that, as economists have proved, the billions of dollars thus extorted by America do nothing to help the well-being of the American people as a whole ... The huge profits are invested in war industries and the main result of its frenzied exploitation of the planet is that the US government is capable of destroying it.

But it was the situation within France which most pre-occupied Beauvoir. Hand in hand with their protests against the American war in Vietnam, students in France and throughout Europe began to attack the hierarchical and authoritarian structure of the educational system. This burgeoned in May 1968 in France into an outright attack on the State itself. Sartre and Beauvoir, former teachers, were all too well acquainted with the iniquities and inadequacies of the educational establishment and their sympathies were wholly with the students, whom the press designated as *enragées*, hotheads, from an early date.

In 1964 *Les Temps Modernes* had already published an article which attacked the system of vast lectures current in French universities and called for a transformation of the relationship between teachers and students. In 1965 a further debate on the question appeared in the magazine. By March 1968 student protests had escalated to such a point that at Nanterre the rector closed the university. From there things moved rapidly and dramatically and by 6 May whole-sale confrontation had erupted between students behind improvised barricades on the left bank and police who behaved like 'hounds on the kill'. The very savagery of police reprisals resulted in the Paris population taking the side of the students. Trade unionists joined the students and called for an unlimited strike and demonstration against the repression, Sartre, together with the psychoanalyst Jacques Lacan, were amongst the signatories of a manifesto which expressed solidarity with the students for 'wishing to escape from an alienated establishment by any means'.

On the evening that this manifesto appeared in *Le Monde*, 10 May, the street fighting reached its crescendo on the left bank. On 12 May, Sartre spoke on Radio Luxembourg, declaring that the students were right not to want to share in a world and a future made by their fathers, those men who were stupefied by obedience and victims of a closed system. His statement, reproduced in tracts which were widely circulated in the Latin Quarter, emphasized that the students' only valid relationship with the university was 'to smash it' and in order to do so they had to come out in the streets. In an interveiw with the student leader, Daniel Cohn-Bendit, which appeared in the *Nouvel Observateur* and served to legitimize Cohn-Bendit's image, Sartre emphasized the need for the movement to continue (despite the proximity of the summer holidays) and particularly the necessity of the students collaborating with the workers.

Both Beauvoir and Sartre, aware, like the student leaders, that the union between workers and students, as well as the revolution, would not be made in a day, nonetheless saw in the student-led uprising an extension of the revolutionary discourse. Poverty and property, the prime movers in previous revolutions, had been replaced by a revolt against systems of power and a demand for self-determination and sovereignty. In *All Said and Done*, Beauvoir writes:

All that the lovers of order had chosen to see in the events of May was a youthful and romantic outburst: the truth of the matter is that these events expressed not the crisis of our generation, but of society as a whole. The students, grown more and more numerous and seeing no future ahead of them, formed the focus at which the contradictions of neo-capitalism exploded: this explosion meant that the entire system was at stake and this directly involved the proletariat.

Beauvoir and Sartre's solidarity with the youth movement did not stop with the May events. They both took on nominal editorship of left papers – Sartre of *La Cause du Peuple*, Simone of *L'Idiot International* – in order to prevent the government from closing these 'subversive' papers down. Their presence as editors brought public and international attention to the repression of freedom such closure entailed. The case of *La Cause du Peuple* is the more notorious one. Run by the Maoist *Gauche prolétarienne*, the paper's editors had been arrested in April 1970 – the first such arrest in France, apart from the period of Occupation, since 1881. Distancing himself from some of the group's analysis, in particular its self-designation as the party of 'Resistance' in a France occupied by the bourgeoisie, Sartre yet took on its 'official' editorship. He should thus have been arrested at once. He wasn't, which suggested, of course, that the paper's previous editors were similarly innocent and should be released from prison. His demand for their release wasn't met: the grouping of the *Gauche prolétarienne* had been banned and the two editors were duly sentenced. In order to bring attention to this injustice, Sartre and Beauvoir held press conferences protesting at the confiscation of a 'legitimate' newspaper, at police violence against the printers of a 'legal' paper and harassment of its distributors. With a group of other celebrities, they took to the streets, giving out copies of the paper and shouting, 'Read *La Cause du Peuple*. Support the freedom of the press.' Not arrested, since the scandal would have been too great, they were instead shepherded off in a police van to have their identities checked. Their special status prevented the arrests of others and showed up the government's self-contradictory actions. Similar actions should bring similar reprisals from the authorities.

During this period Beauvoir and Sartre lent their support to other left causes. One was the famous case of the alleged incendiaries, said to have tossed Molotov cocktails into the managers' offices of a mine where a recent explosion had resulted in the deaths of sixteen miners. The police summarily rounded up four Maoists and two criminals and accused them of the bombing. Parallel to their trial, Sartre headed a tribunal which indicted the local authority and the 'state as employer' for the accident which had killed the sixteen miners and for an exploitative system of production which forced miners to forego necessary safety precautions. As one witness at the tribunal evocatively pointed out, 'If you keep to the safety regulations . . . your children will never eat meat.'

Around this time, Beauvoir wrote an investigative exposé of a purported industrial accident at a factory which packed gaseous substances for use in insecticides and beauty products. Of its largely female work force, three had been killed and the rest permanently handicapped and disfigured by a particularly terrible explosion. Beauvoir's article showed how labour inspectors, doctors and courts were in league with employers, allowing them to get away with conditions which effectively resulted in murder. 'In eighty per cent of factories in France,' Beauvoir writes, 'safety is sacrificed to profit and the workers risk their lives every day.'

Her investigative work brought home to Simone how necessary it was for the persecuted left-wing press to exist: '. . . no one else troubles to give a truthful, detailed account of the workers' state, their daily life and their struggles. The *gauchiste* papers do try to tell the workers what is happening within their own class – a subject that the bourgeois press ignores or misrepresents.'

Although her sympathies with the Maoists in France in these years did not extend to a blind faith in China, or in an imminent revolution, she found herself in agreement with them on a number of points. Unlike the traditional left-wing, the Maoists denied the existing system wholeheartedly. They focused on those 'fresh forces' the unions paid little attention to – the young, the women, the foreigners and unorganized labour; and they encouraged action. In *All Said and Done*, she writes, 'I should rather try to help the young in their struggle than be the passive witness of a despair that has led some of them to the most hideous suicide.'

In certain respects Beauvoir and Sartre's alliance with the young echoes her sense of old age as an absurd parody of former life. The scores of photographs which depict Simone and a frail Sartre in the ranks of young demonstrators or on street corners selling newspapers have a note of the ridiculous about them as well as of pathos. No longer at the centre of events, initiators integral to their history, Sartre and Beauvoir were famous names, called in to bring media attention to various causes, to pose for the cameras. There is a sad inevitability to this, yet in the balance, their willingness to respond to the young, their openness to change, remains admirable.

In the course of the 1970s, the revolutionary left lost impetus in France. However there was one movement with which Beauvoir allied herself which took on increasing momentum: feminism. Here, her presence in the ranks has nothing of parody. *The Second Sex* marked a point of origin for the women's movement and was integral to the development of modern feminism and its analysis of the condition of women.

At the time that she wrote *The Second Sex*, however, Beauvoir was self-avowedly not a feminist. The book is not a militant one. Nor does it in any central way call for solidarity amongst women. In the aftermath of World War II, Beauvoir felt that much had already changed for the better in the situation of women and that their state would evolve with that of society as a whole. When she commented in *Force of Circumstance* that she wished she had given the book a materialist foundation and based the rejection and oppression of the 'Other' on an economic explanation, she was still not a feminist. Rather, her political orientation had shifted further to the left. Women's situation, she thought, depended on the future of labour in the world and would change only 'at the price of an upheaval in the forces of production'. By 1970 her position had grown far more radical: 'Now when I speak of feminism I mean the fact of struggling for specifically feminine claims at the same time as carrying on the class war.'

In an interview with the journalist Alice Schwarzer which was published in the *Nouvel Observateur* in 1972, Beauvoir explains the reasons for her change in mind and heart:

The situation of woman in France has not really changed over the last twenty years. She has benefited from a few small things on the legal level where marriage and divorce are concerned. The use of contraceptives has spread, but in an insufficient manner, since only 7 per cent of French women use the pill. Neither have there been any specific gains in the sphere of work. There are perhaps a few more women who work than before, but not many. In any case, they're confined to positions of little importance . . .

Beauvoir goes on to say that she had no wish to associate herself with the reformist and legalistically based women's movements that existed prior to 1970. But the new feminism, the MLF (Mouvement de Libération des Femmes), was radical and took up the challenge of 1968 'to change life as of today; not to count on the future, but to act without waiting'. Most importantly, she adds, 'I recognized that it is necessary, before the socialism we dream of arrives, to struggle for the actual position of women . . . Even in socialist countries, this equality hasn't been obtained. Women must therefore take their destiny into their own hands.'

This interview, translated into many languages, gained in significance because it appeared at the very moment when women were affirming the separateness of their claims against those of the various left movements in which they had participated. Beauvoir's emphasis on the fact that a social revolution would not necessarily alter women's condition, that even within the left groups in France, there was a profound inequality between men and women – all this served to consolidate what many women felt and had experienced.

Simone's new militant feminism took concrete form in 1970. Approached by a group of the MLF who were campaigning to legalize abortion in France, Beauvoir agreed to sign her name to a manifesto which proclaimed, 'I have had an abortion and I demand this right for all women.' The *Manifesto of the 343*, as it came to be known (some, but not all of them famous women), was published in the *Nouvel Observateur* in the spring of 1971. This gesture of solidarity marked a beginning for Simone. From then on she marched in support of freedom of motherhood, birth control and abortion and against crimes against women; she lent her name to any number of activities and her flat to the first 'feminist' abortions. She met regularly with a group of feminists and although she never strayed from that formality and politeness which were part of her background, her presence was a warm and enthusiastic one. She read widely of the new feminist literature from all over the world and corresponded regularly with feminists in many countries. In 1974 she suggested the creation of 'The League of Women's Rights' of which she was president for many years. *Les Temps Modernes*, under her impetus, devoted a special issue to women and from 1973 on carried a special section on 'le sexisme quotidien' – everyday sexism.

Some of Beauvoir's ideas changed in response to the women's movement. Others remained untouched. She continued to insist that men had a part to play in the liberation of women – and thus of themselves – and was adamantly opposed to notions of separatism which would shut women into a 'feminine ghetto'. Her feelings about the slavery which motherhood imposes, about the mystification of motherhood by men and the state in order to trap women into dependency, remained strong.

The basic tenet of *The Second Sex* – that you are not born a woman, you become one – was hers until her death. She was opposed to that feminist thinking which championed specifically feminine qualities, values or ways of life:

to believe this would mean acknowledging the existence of a specifically female nature – that is to say agreeing with a myth invented by men to confine women to their oppressed state. For women it is not a question of asserting themselves as women, but of becoming full-scale human beings.

And that meant not rejecting all of culture because it is male, but 'taking over the tools forged by men for our own interests'.

Any positions which hinted at an eternal feminine were anathema to Beauvoir. In a 1976 interview with Alice Schwarzer she commented:

It's a good thing that woman should no longer be ashamed of her body, her pregnancy, her periods. That she gets to know her body, I find excellent . . . But it isn't necessary to make a value of that and believe that the female body gives you a new vision of the world. That would be ridiculous and absurd; it would be to erect a counter-penis. Women who share this belief fall back into the irrational, the mystical, the cosmic. They play into men's hands and they can then oppress them more easily, more easily exclude them from knowledge and power. The eternal feminine is a lie; nature plays an infinitesimal role in the development of a human being. We are social beings. Because I don't believe that woman is naturally inferior to man, I also do not believe that she is naturally superior.

Beauvoir's emphasis gives priority to the rational and the social. Yet with the critical clarity which she aimed as much

163

at herself as at the world, she remained until the end far more open to new movements, both social and intellectual, than even the age-defying Sartre. She read the new structuralist thinkers who had displaced the existentialists at the centre of French intellectual life. At the age of sixty-eight, in 1976, she stated that she would willingly undertake a new study of psychoanalysis from a feminist viewpoint. She remarked that if she were to rewrite her autobiography, she would be far more open about her experience of sexuality, which she now recognised as a political as well as an individual question.

With tireless energy in these last years, Beauvoir debated with and personally answered scores of letters from women around the world who saw her as the doyenne of this new wave of feminism. She took part in several films and gave numerous interviews aimed at helping her public know her better and at giving voice to a cause to which she was profoundly attached. Beauvoirian centres for women's studies sprang up in Canada and the United States, and in Paris the Centre Audiovisuel Simone de Beavuoir was set up. With Sylvie Le Bon, Beauvoir travelled to the US and spent some days on the feminist Kate Millett's farm where a conversation between then was filmed. She was named head of a government commission on women and culture and she met regularly, along with other feminists, with the Minister for Women's Rights in President Mitterand's government.

While Simone's health held up through these years, permitting her to work on the whole without flagging, from 1970 on Sartre's took a dramatic turn for the worse. Indeed, the testimony of *Adieux: A Farewell to Sartre* leads me to suspect that it was Sartre's old age which weighed on

Simone almost more than her own. From 1970, when *Old Age* appeared, through the period when she was writing the last volume of her memoirs published in 1972, until Sartre's death in 1980, Simone's life centred on the care of a failing Sartre. It was she who stage-managed the complicated comings and goings of that retinue of people who looked after Sartre in his last years of blindness and infirmity. These included long-established women friends, his adopted daughter Arlette Elkaim, inheritor of his estate, and Benny Lévy – the one person on whom his and Simone's life-long relationship all but foundered. Every week Sartre would spend two nights at Arlette's home and the remaining nights at Simone's. In the mornings he worked with Lévy and most afternoons Simone worked at his flat. Everything was done to allow Sartre to maintain his self-respect, despite his failing senses.

The Benny Lévy story is a disputed one. From Beauvoir's point of view, this young hyper-intelligent, but unscrupulous Maoist, whose intellectual development led him to embrace a mystical Judaism, had – by the sheer brilliance and energy of his youthful disputations – won an ailing Sartre over, only then to inveigle him into what amounted to a renunciation of all his former thought. Together old philosopher and young philosopher were preparing a book on power and freedom, based on their conversations. Just before Sartre's death, a conversation of this kind was published in the *Nouvel Observateur*. Simone, already at odds with Lévy over a previous unprinted piece and because he treated the entire *Les Temps Modernes* team as corpses, was shown the article before it appeared. She writes:

I was horrified. It had nothing to do with the plural thought that Sartre had spoken of . . . Victor [Benny Lévy] did not express any of his own opinions directly; he made Sartre assume them while he, by virtue of who knows what revealed truth, played the part of district attorney. The tone in which he spoke to Sartre and his arrogant superiority utterly disgusted all the friends who saw the document before it was published. And like me they were horrified by the nature of the statements extorted from Sartre.

Her sense of betrayal at Sartre's allowing the piece to appear against her advice was acute.

As Simone was ready to recognize, Lévy had, for Sartre, a different meaning than for her. His eyes always fixed on the future, the dying Sartre saw in Lévy the new intellectual of whom he dreamed. In a sense, too, Lévy was the living prolongation of himself. On a more practical level, he also provided the regular intellectual stimulus which none of Sartre's older collaborators, too enmeshed in their own lives, were prepared to give.

There is no doubt that Simone was at once angered by an influence on Sartre which prevailed over hers and saddened by the existence of a relationship which split them apart more than any other had done. Simone had even painfully managed to come to terms with Sartre's adoption of his young former mistress, Arlette Elkaim, who was to become his literary executor in place of Simone. It may well have been that this act of Sartre's influenced her in her decision formally to adopt Sylvie Le Bon. But over Benny Lévy, there was no recourse. The generational struggle had displaced Simone more effectively than any lovers' battle.

In 1976, when the rupture over Lévy first took place,

Sartre talked of going to silent dinners with his 'stern muses' Sylvie and Simone. There is a sense in which the taped conversations with Sartre dating from the summer of 1974 and published as part of Beauvoir's *Adieux*, are her attempt to reinstate the 'true', the living Sartre to which his work and Simone's autobiography had created a monument.

This final misunderstanding between them notwithstanding, Beauvoir's *Adieux: A Farewell to Sartre* remains along with *A Very Easy Death*, her most devastatingly moving book. It is almost too raw, too painful in its testimony, too frank in its detail of a humiliating decline. Simone had lost her life-long companion. As she noted: 'This is the first of my books – the only one no doubt – that you will not have read before it is printed. It is wholly and entirely devoted to you; and you are not affected by it . . . Even if I am buried next to you there will be no communication between your ashes and mine.'

Despite her formidable activity over the next six years, her numerous trips, interviews, and editorial tasks, including her preparation for publication of Sartre's *Lettres au Castor*, Simone wrote no more books. Death had been her subject for many years. In this most exemplary of lives, it was appropriately the last.

Simone de Beauvoir died in Paris on 14 April 1986.

Selected Bibliography

Simone de Beauvoir's principal works are listed here. I give the date of the original edition, followed by the date of translation into English and then the most easily accessible British edition: this last is usually the translation used in the text.

L'Invitée, Gallimard, Paris, 1943. *She Came to Stay* (1949), Flamingo, London, 1984.

Pyrrhus et Cinéas, Gallimard, Paris, 1944.

Le sang des autres, Gallimard, Paris, 1945. *The Blood of Others* (1948), Penguin Books, Harmondsworth, 1984.

Les bouches inutiles, Gallimard, Paris, 1945. (First performed at the Théatre des Carrefours in Paris in October 1945.)

Tous les hommes sont mortels, Gallimard, Paris, 1945. *All Men are Mortal*, World Publishing Company, Cleveland, 1955.

Pour une morale de l'ambiguité, Gallimard, Paris, 1947. *The Ethics of Ambiguity*, Philosophical Library, New York, 1948.

L'Amérique au jour le jour, Morihien, Paris, 1948. *America Day By Day*, Duckworth, London, 1957.

Le deuxième sexe, Gallimard, Paris, 1949. *The Second Sex* (1953), Penguin, Harmondsworth, 1983.

Les Mandarins, Gallimard, Paris, 1954. *The Mandarins* (1957), Flamingo, London, 1982.

Privilèges, Gallimard, Paris, 1955.

La longue marche, Gallimard, Paris, 1957. *The Long March*, André Deutsch/Weidenfeld & Nicolson, London, 1958.

Memoires d'une jeune fille rangée, Gallimard, Paris, 1958. *Memoirs of a Dutiful Daughter* (1959), Penguin, Harmondsworth, 1963.

La force de l'âge, Gallimard, Paris, 1960. *The Prime of Life* (1962), Penguin, Harmondsworth, 1965.

Brigitte Bardot and the Lolita Syndrome, André Deutsch/ Weidenfeld & Nicolson, London, 1960.

Preface to Gisèle Halimi *Djamila Boupacha*, Gallimard, Paris, 1962; Four Square Books, London, 1963.

La force des choses, Gallimard, Paris, 1963. *Force of Circumstance.* (1965) Penguin, Harmondsworth, 1968.

Une mort très douce, Gallimard, Paris, 1964. *A Very Easy Death* (1966), Penguin, Harmondsworth, 1969.

Les belles images, Gallimard, Paris, 1966. *Les Belles Images* (1968), Flamingo, London, 1985.

La femme rompue, Gallimard, Paris, 1968. *The Woman Destroyed* (1969), Flamingo, London, 1984.

La vieillesse, Gallimard, Paris, 1970. *Old Age* (1972), Penguin, Harmondsworth, 1977.

Tout compte fait, Gallimard, Paris, 1972. *All Said and Done* (1974) Penguin, Harmondsworth, 1977.

Quand prime le spirituel, Gallimard, Paris, 1979. *When Things of the Spirit Come First* (1982), Flamingo, London, 1983.

La céremonie des adieux suivi des Entretiens avec Jean-Paul Sartre, Gallimard, Paris, 1981. *Adieux: A Farwell to Sartre* (1984), Penguin, Harmondsworth, 1985.

Lettres au Castor et à quelques autres by Jean-Paul Sartre, edited by Simone de Beauvoir, Gallimard, Paris, 1983.

There have been several books and a great many essays, particularly in recent years, devoted to Simone de Beauvoir's life and work. The most recent biography by Claude Francis and Fernande Gontier (Perrin, Paris, 1985) is highly readable but somewhat romanticized. Francis and Gontier have also produced an excellent compendium of previously unpublished texts and uncollected shorter pieces, *Les écrits de Simone de Beauvoir* (Gallimard, Paris, 1979). Alice Schwarzer's *Simone de Beauvoir Today: Conversations 1972–1982* provides a fascinating insight into Beauvoir's position *vis-à-vis* contemporary feminism.

Of the many feminist analyses of Beauvoir's work, Margaret Walters's 'The Rights and Wrongs of Women' in the book by that title (edited by Ann Oakley and Juliet Mitchell, Penguin, 1976) and Juliet Mitchell's chapter on Beauvoir in *Psychoanalysis and Feminism* (Penguin, 1975), as well as Elizabeth Wilson's in *Hidden Agendas* (Methuen, 1986) are particularly resonant. Ann Whitmarsh in *Simone de Beauvoir and the Limits of Commitment* (Cambridge University Press, 1981) presents a thorough analysis of Beauvoir's existentialist project. Mary Evans's *Simone de Beauvoir: A Feminist Mandarin* (Tavistock, 1985) is a sympathetic and well-rounded study. Judith Okely's book, *Simone de Beauvoir: A Re-reading*, in the Virago Pioneers series offers an appraisal of Beauvoir's contribution by juxtaposing a pre-feminist 1960s' reading with a contemporary one.

Two recent biographies of Jean-Paul Sartre, Annie Cohen-Solal, *Sartre* (Gallimard, 1985) and Ronald Hayman, *Writing Against* (Weidenfeld & Nicolson, 1986) present an alternative perspective on the Sartre-Beauvoir relationship to that of Beauvoir's autobiography. Sartre's *Les Carnets de la drôle de guerre* (Gallimard, Paris, 1983), translated as *War Diaries* (Verso, 1984), is also interesting in this light.

FOR THE BEST IN PAPERBACKS, LOOK FOR THE

In every corner of the world, on every subject under the sun, Penguin represents quality and variety – the very best in publishing today.

For complete information about books available from Penguin – including Pelicans, Puffins, Peregrines and Penguin Classics – and how to order them, write to us at the appropriate address below. Please note that for copyright reasons the selection of books varies from country to country.

In the United Kingdom: For a complete list of books available from Penguin in the U.K., please write to *Dept E.P., Penguin Books Ltd, Harmondsworth, Middlesex, UB7 0DA*

In the United States: For a complete list of books available from Penguin in the U.S., please write to *Dept BA, Penguin, 299 Murray Hill Parkway, East Rutherford, New Jersey 07073*

In Canada: For a complete list of books available from Penguin in Canada, please write to *Penguin Books Canada Ltd, 2801 John Street, Markham, Ontario L3R 1B4*

In Australia: For a complete list of books available from Penguin in Australia, please write to the *Marketing Department, Penguin Books Australia Ltd, P.O. Box 257, Ringwood, Victoria 3134*

In New Zealand: For a complete list of books available from Penguin in New Zealand, please write to the *Marketing Department, Penguin Books (NZ) Ltd, Private Bag, Takapuna, Auckland 9*

In India: For a complete list of books available from Penguin, please write to *Penguin Overseas Ltd, 706 Eros Apartments, 56 Nehru Place, New Delhi, 110019*

In Holland: For a complete list of books available from Penguin in Holland, please write to *Penguin Books Nederland B.V., Postbus 195, NL–1380AD Weesp, Netherlands*

In Germany: For a complete list of books available from Penguin, please write to *Penguin Books Ltd, Friedrichstrasse 10 – 12, D–6000 Frankfurt Main 1, Federal Republic of Germany*

In Spain: For a complete list of books available from Penguin in Spain, please write to *Longman Penguin España, Calle San Nicolas 15, E–28013 Madrid, Spain*

FOR THE BEST IN PAPERBACKS, LOOK FOR THE 🐧

PENGUIN MODERN CLASSICS

The Age of Reason   Jean-Paul Sartre

The first part of Sartre's classic trilogy, set in the volatile Paris summer of 1938, is itself 'a dynamic, deeply disturbing novel' (Elizabeth Bowen) which tackles some of the major issues of our time.

Three Lives   Gertrude Stein

A turning point in American literature, these portraits of three women – thin, worn Anna, patient, gentle Lena and the complicated, intelligent Melanctha – represented in 1909 one of the pioneering examples of modernist writing.

Doctor Faustus   Thomas Mann

Perhaps the most convincing description of an artistic genius ever written, this portrait of the composer Leverkuhn is a classic statement of one of Mann's obsessive themes: the discord between genius and sanity.

The New Machiavelli   H. G. Wells

This autobiography of a man who has thrown up a glittering political career and marriage to go into exile with the woman he loves also contains an illuminating Introduction by Melvyn Bragg.

The Collected Poems of Stevie Smith

Amused, amusing and deliciously barbed, this volume includes many poems which dwell on death; as a whole, though, as this first complete edition in paperback makes clear, Smith's poetry affirms an irrepressible love of life.

Rhinoceros / The Chairs / The Lesson   Eugène Ionesco

Three great plays by the man who was one of the founders of what has come to be known as the Theatre of the Absurd.

The Second Sex   Simone de Beauvoir

This great study of Woman is a landmark in feminist history, drawing together insights from biology, history and sociology as well as literature, psychoanalysis and mythology to produce one of the supreme classics of the twentieth century.

The Bridge of San Luis Rey   Thornton Wilder

On 20 July 1714 the finest bridge in all Peru collapsed, killing 5 people. Why? Did it reveal a latent pattern in human life? In this beautiful, vivid and compassionate investigation, Wilder asks some searching questions in telling the story of the survivors.

Parents and Children   Ivy Compton-Burnett

This richly entertaining introduction to the world of a unique novelist brings to light the deadly claustrophobia within a late-Victorian upper-middle-class family . . .

Vienna 1900   Arthur Schnitzler

These deceptively languid sketches, four 'games with love and death', lay bare an astonishing and disturbing world of sexual turmoil (which anticipates Freud's discoveries) beneath the smooth surface of manners and convention.

Confessions of Zeno   Italo Svevo

Zeno, an innocent in a corrupt world, triumphs in the end through his stoic acceptance of his own failings in this extraordinary, experimental novel which fuses memory, obsession and desire.

The House of Mirth   Edith Wharton

Lily Bart – beautiful, intelligent and charming – is trapped like a butterfly in the inverted jam jar of wealthy New York society . . . This tragic comedy of manners was one of Wharton's most shocking and innovative books.

BIOGRAPHY AND AUTOBIOGRAPHY IN PENGUIN

Jackdaw Cake Norman Lewis

From Carmarthen to Cuba, from Enfield to Algeria, Norman Lewis brilliantly recounts his transformation from stammering schoolboy to the man Auberon Waugh called 'the greatest travel writer alive, if not the greatest since Marco Polo'.

Catherine Maureen Dunbar

Catherine is the tragic story of a young woman who died of anorexia nervosa. Told by her mother, it includes extracts from Catherine's diary and conveys both the physical and psychological traumas suffered by anorexics.

Isak Dinesen, the Life of Karen Blixen Judith Thurman

Myth-spinner and storyteller famous far beyond her native Denmark, Karen Blixen lived much of the Gothic strangeness of her tales. This remarkable biography paints Karen Blixen in all her sybiline beauty and magnetism, conveying the delight and terror she inspired, and the pain she suffered.

The Silent Twins Marjorie Wallace

June and Jennifer Gibbons are twenty-three year old identical twins, who from childhood have been locked together in a strange secret bondage which made them reject the outside world. *The Silent Twins* is a real-life psychological thriller about the most fundamental question – what makes a separate, individual human being?

Backcloth Dirk Bogarde

The final volume of Dirk Bogarde's autobiography is not about his acting years but about Dirk Bogarde the man and the people and events that have shaped his life and character. All are remembered with affection, nostalgia and characteristic perception and eloquence.